EFFECTIVE TIME MANAGEMENT

HOW TO SAVE TIME AND
SPEND IT WISELY

JOHN ADAIR

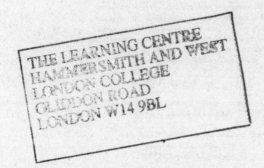
PAN BOOKS

First published 1982 by The Talbot Adair Press

This edition published 2009 by Pan Books
an imprint of Pan Macmillan Ltd
Pan Macmillan, 20 New Wharf Road, London N1 9RR
Basingstoke and Oxford
Associated companies throughout the world
www.panmacmillan.com

ISBN 978-0-330-50424-9

A CIP catalogue record for this book is available from
the British Library.

Typeset by SetSystems Ltd, Saffron Walden, Essex
Printed and bound in the UK by
CPI Mackays, Chatham ME5 8TD

Visit **www.panmacmillan.com** to read more about all our books
and to buy them. You will also find features, author interviews and
news of any author events, and you can sign up for e-newsletters
so that you're always first to hear about our new releases.

EFFECTIVE TIME MANAGEMENT

Educated at St Paul's School, London, John Adair has enjoyed a varied and colourful career. He served in the Arab Legion, worked as a deckhand on an Arctic trawler and had a spell as an orderly in a hospital operating theatre. After graduating from Cambridge, he became Senior Lecturer in Military History and Leadership Training Adviser at the Royal Military Academy, Sandhurst, before becoming Director of Studies at St George's House in Windsor Castle and then Associate Director of The Industrial Society.

In 1979 John became the world's first university professor of Leadership Studies at the University of Surrey. He holds the degrees of Master of Arts from Cambridge University, Master of Letters from Oxford University and Doctor of Philosophy from London University, and he also is a Fellow of the Royal Historical Society.

In 2006 the People's Republic of China conferred on John the title of Honorary Professor of Leadership Studies in recognition of his 'outstanding research and contribution in the field of Leadership'. In 2009 the United Nations appointed him as Chair of Strategic Leadership Studies at its central college in Turin.

John has written over forty books on leadership, management and history, which have been translated into many languages.

www.johnadair.co.uk

'Nothing really belongs to us but time,
which even he has who has nothing else.'

Baltasar Gracian, Spanish writer

'Time wasted is existence, used is life.'

Edward Young, English poet

For Katharine, James and Edmund

CONTENTS

FOREWORD

'Time wasted is existence, used is life.'
Edward Young

Since this book was first published in 1987 under the title of *How To Manage Your Time* there has been an explosion of interest in time management. Google, for example, offers you around 130 million items under that heading. Just as we are suffering from information overload from the media and Internet, not to mention constant emails and often intrusive mobile telephone calls and texts, so we are being offered ever more advice often from very self-interested sources about how to solve all our problems of time.

Only someone with their head in the sand like an ostrich would deny that there are such time problems. Balancing all the real demands on your time, however skilled you are at 'multi-tasking', is not always easy. This is especially true if you are a single parent or part of a family where both partners work.

Technological innovations such as those mentioned above can of course save us time in a wonderful way. But they can also be time management minefields. There are people, for example, whose time is hopelessly fragmented by mindless responses to every email that comes across their screen. There are even addicts to mobile phones and texting who have forever lost complete solitude or time to think.

In fact your salvation doesn't lie in technology at all, not even in the original innovation of clocks and watches that are now quartz-accurate to the second. Technology makes a good servant to humanity but a very bad master. What gives us a degree of control over our time is a combination of reflective thinking and clear thinking. If you are willing to invest some time in those two activities, then you will, I trust, find this book to be a helpful guide and an encouraging companion.

You will notice that the book has a simple framework – the Ten Principles of Time Management – as summarized at the back. These are the fundamentals or basics of the subject, the ones that you need to graft into your mind, so that they are as much a part of you as the air that you breathe.

Some of the principles require reflective thinking on your part, especially those concerned with time and life. That leads on to reflections about your own values, the 'stars' you steer your life by. Although we are hardly aware of it, these values are the major determinants in almost all our choices or decisions. How we spend our time is the expression of them.

Now it is impossible and unnecessary to be too precise about values, your own or other people's, but you should at least have a good working knowledge of what is important or significant for you in life and what is not. Others may see it differently but you are you. Our first calling is always to be ourselves – well, our best selves.

Reflective thinking will take you thus far but it won't take you all the way – you also need to be able to think clearly about the daily tactics of time management. As I shall leave you to discover, most of the Ten Principles are really invitations to do some clear thinking about your purpose, aims and objectives, about what business you are in and what business you are not in, about the policies that can save you time in decision making when in repetitive situations. You will find, too, that I stress the importance of the skill of being able to make plans that are both definite and flexible. That is a necessary condition for being effective in any field of life.

May I add lastly my hope that you will find inspiration in these pages as well as principles, strategies, techniques, systems, rules of thumb and practical tips. For you will not become a master of your time overnight. It is a long journey, one with plenty of uphills and downhills, dark valleys and dry deserts. May this book be for you a well of continual inspiration, a source of hope and encouragement that will keep you ever moving forwards on the journey.

John Adair, 2009

The wood is lovely, dark and deep,
But I have promises to keep,
And miles to go before I sleep.
Robert Frost, US poet

1

TIME MANAGEMENT IN PERSPECTIVE

'What is time? How did the concept of time management arise? What is the relation of time management to life as a whole?'

These are not easy questions to answer. Possibly for that reason they are ignored by most other books on time management. Let us not make that mistake. For the attempt to view time management in its historical perspective may yield some important insights.

This chapter invites you to identify your assumptions about time management. How far are they *your* beliefs, consciously adopted and held? You may find that some of them are more or less unconscious assumptions, picked up from our common history and culture. For we inherit a tradition. It helps if we understand that tradition and build upon the foundations.

THE NATURE OF TIME

A sense of time as transitory is deeply human. As far as we know animals do not experience it. *Tempus fugit* – time flies

- is a universal refrain. But what is time? Ancient philosophers were as much puzzled as we are:

> For what is Time? Who is able easily and briefly to explain it? Who is able so much as to comprehend it in thought as to express himself concerning it? And yet what in our usual discourse do we more familiarly and knowingly make more mention of than Time? And surely we understand it well enough when we speak of it; we understand it also when in speaking with another we hear it named. What then is Time? If nobody asks me I know; but if I wanted to explain it to someone that should ask me, plainly I do not know.
>
> **St. Augustine, philosopher and theologian (354–430)**

In terms of our definition of time, things have not changed much since St. Augustine wrote those words. We all know what we mean by time but we cannot say what it is. Philosophers and physicists are less sure, for their speculations and calculations have not yet thrown more light on the matter.

If you are travelling at a speed faster than another person, time will go slower for you. If you flew around the world at 500 miles per hour with an atomic clock on the seat beside you, when you returned to where you started your clock would be about one hundredth of a millionth of a second slower than its twin on the ground.

Albert Einstein's discovery of this relativity provoked much thought about the relations of the dimensions of time and space. At very great speeds time does go slower. For general or everyday purposes, however, Einstein's discovery adds nothing to our understanding of time, for we don't travel at the kind of speed he had in mind. But Einstein has added to the mystery of time.

The nearest we can come to grasping the concept of time is to look upon it as a dimension, like space: *it is the dimension in which change happens.* The rate of change varies enormously: mountains form and crumble over millions of years while men are born and die over decades. Being human we tend to measure time and change in terms of our life span.

Although we know that each hour has sixty minutes and each minute sixty seconds we experience time in different ways. Sometimes we are not aware of it at all. Sometimes it goes faster and sometimes slower. Time has its own psychology.

'No young man believes he shall ever die,' wrote the literary critic and philosopher William Hazlitt. There is a feeling of eternity in youth; perhaps the young are prodigal with time because they feel they have so much of it. Yet boredom, not knowing what to do with time, can be the other side of the coin.

As we advance in life we acquire a keener sense of the value of time. For some people nothing else seems of any consequence; and in this respect they become misers. But for others time can again hang heavy. For a very old person sitting in hospital waiting to go home time can seem like eternity. Yet for such a person, paradoxically, there may be only days or hours of time left.

Time often seems to me to go more slowly in the dark than in the light, just as time waiting to see the dentist or for a train to arrive can drag its feet.

There are other illusions. Generally, when we are looking forward intensely to something, the *shorter* the time the *longer* it seems to us. Is that because we measure it in shorter units? Or simply because we are conscious of time and think about measuring it?

Time spent in purposeful activity can fly past. That may

be why, as we grow older, time can seem to be speeding up – years go by faster, days are like hours, and hours minutes. Providing we are busy, that is.

Perhaps this is why time management is most likely to be attractive to busy people.

A CLOCKWORK REVOLUTION

The ordinary man is not bothered by our comparative ignorance about the nature of time. What matters to him is that he can measure time. If, like the great majority of the world's population, in this century as in previous ones, he lives by farming or herding, his time is measured for him by natural events: dawn, sunrise, high noon, sunset and night-fall. He needs no more accurate measure for his daily activities. We all live by nature's clock. Day follows night; season follows season. These cycles are stamped upon us.

Why, then, do we need clocks? Who needs them? Even the most ancient and most natural of artificial clocks – the sundial – can seem an intruder on the business of living. In his history of time measurement *Revolution in Time* (1983) David Landes quotes an actor's amusing lament from a play performed in ancient Rome:

> The gods confound the man who first found out
> How to distinguish hours. Confound him, too,
> Who in this place set up a sundial,
> To cut and hack my days so wretchedly
> Into small pieces! When I was a boy,
> My belly was my sundial – one surer,
> Truer, and more exact than any of them.
> This dial told me when 'twas the proper time
> To go to dinner, when I ought to eat,

> But nowadays, why even when I have,
> I can't fall to unless the sun gives leave.
> The town's so full of these confounded dials . . .

The sundial as a form of clock had grave limitations. It would not work in countries where clouds obscured the sun for much of the year. By the end of the fourteenth century some ingenious Europeans succeeded in inventing mechanical clocks complete with a series of gear wheels driven by weights. Fitted only with an hour hand and lacking in accuracy they yet served both to show the time and strike it out on bells in churches and city squares. The clock next to St. Mark's Cathedral in Venice is a fine surviving example.

Gradually clocks became smaller until relatively wealthy people could own a portable clock for domestic use. The key technological step was the invention of the coiled spring, which could be made even smaller. From table clocks the European craftsmen developed the pocket watch. Not until the 1860s did the Swiss mass-produce a reliable cheap watch for the man in the street; not until the First World War did wristwatches become popular.

Meanwhile clocks became ever more accurate, measuring minutes and seconds. John Harrison's marine chronometer lost or gained no more than one second a day by the time it was fully honed in the mid-eighteenth century. Only the relatively recent introduction of quartz technology has brought that degree of accuracy to the common household clock and wristwatch. The use of quartz means that we can now personally measure our time in seconds. Today's atomic clocks are even more accurate than that.

TIME DISCIPLINE

A commercial sense of time – time is money – seems to have been born among the Italian merchants of the late Middle Ages. It was mixed with the religious concern inculcated by the Church and heightened by the haunting imminence of death. Few reached their allotted span of three score years and ten.

The Black Death wiped out between a quarter and a third of the population in the fourteenth century; also the century when mechanical clocks made their first appearance. Life was short and uncertain: death stood at one's shoulder. Therefore time must be used to the full.

Leon Alberti was a partner in a firm of Italian merchants in the early fifteenth century whose correspondence has survived. From his letters it is clear that young Alberti deserves to be recognized as a pioneer of modern time management.

'In the morning when I get up,' he wrote, 'the first thing I do is think to myself: what am I going to do today? So many things: I count them, think about them, and to each I assign its time.' He continued, 'I'd rather lose sleep than time, in the sense of the proper time for doing what has to be done.'

Sleeping, eating and the like could always be done tomorrow but not so with today's business. Alberti set himself 'to watch the time, and assign things by time, to devote oneself to business and never lose an hour of time'.

With the excitement of a man who has glimpsed a great truth he concludes: 'He who knows how not to waste time can do just about anything; and he who knows how to make use of time will be lord of whatever he wants.'

The English Puritan preachers in particular gave practical instructions in plain language to their congregations on how to save time and use it. For example they advocated the keeping of journals or diaries as a means of daily self-examination, thereby creating a practical time management tool. They advocated the daily planning of time and lay Puritans heeded the message. Sir Matthew Hale, a Puritan judge in Restoration England, followed his daily morning prayers by sitting down and making a careful plan for the day ahead.

It is no surprise then that Protestants led the way in the manufacture of pocket watches, especially in France and Switzerland. Where people had once relied upon the night watchman's cry, the tolling of church bells, or the striking turret clock in the market square, now they could *watch* the time at home or on their person. Lives could not be ordered in a style once reserved for monastic communities. Time had become more personal.

All those activities that depend on people meeting and parting could now be organized by the clock. Generals could synchronize the great movements of troops; railways could be run in accordance with complicated timetables. None of this was possible before the widespread use of clocks and watches.

'Remember that time is money,' wrote US Founding Father Benjamin Franklin in *Advice to a Young Tradesman* (1748). In 1723 Franklin had run away from his Puritan parents in New England, but not before he had imbibed the Puritan virtues of thrift, industry and conscientiousness. The sons and grandsons of the Puritans, breathing the more secular air of the eighteenth century, did not abandon the principle of managing time. They changed the ends. In place of the glory and enjoyment of God in this world and the next, they substituted the mundane pursuits of wealth, health and happiness. 'Do you love life?' said Franklin. 'Then do not squander time, for that is the stuff life is made of.'

TIME IS LIKE MONEY

Time discipline, then, can be applied to any ends. It is a transferable skill. In history there has been a shift from religious to secular ends – especially in the making of money. This is not irreversible. There is no reason why the principles of time management now taught in a business context cannot be applied to spiritual and intellectual life. For example, the businessman's proverb – 'time is money' – can help us towards a personal philosophy of time.

Human understanding advances partly by the use of analogy. This is especially true when it comes to talking about such abstractions as time. Franklin was not the first to compare time to money, but since his day it has become the most common analogy. It is worth reflecting carefully about it.

Both time and money are limited resources. That's the point of the analogy. Therefore time (like money) is a valuable commodity. It can be borrowed, saved or squandered – all words springing from the original and basic analogy. Indeed there is a whole system of smaller metaphors under the 'time is money' umbrella, such as:

> Yesterday is a cancelled cheque
> Tomorrow is a promissory note
> Today is ready cash. Use it!

The invention of banks, virtually unknown in Puritan days, adds another dimension to the analogy. Many of our forefathers pictured 'Time' as a bald old man with a forelock, carrying a scythe and an hourglass. Perhaps today we would imagine Father Time as a bank manager, threatening us with notice of our impending bankruptcy and turning towards us a digital clock.

All analogies break down at a certain point. Time is patently *not* money. It is only when we begin to think about the ways in which it is not money that our sense of its uniqueness comes home. You can make money; you can't make time. Money isn't finite. Sand in the hourglass is not like money in the bank. As the Chinese proverb says: 'An inch of gold cannot buy an inch of time.' Time really is infinitely *more* precious than money.

The 'time is money' analogy is operational, not a mere literary ornament. It is a positive and practical help to look upon time as money. For money is a widespread yardstick of value. If we see our time as being *more* valuable than money we have it about right. As most of us try to save our money and invest it wisely, how much more should we try to avoid wasting our time and to invest it with energy to good effect?

Arnold Bennett's book *How to Live on Twenty-Four Hours a Day* (1907), ran through fourteen editions in the US. Although Bennett was mainly concerned in proving that a clerk commuting daily to the City of London could find plenty of time to read good books if he chose to manage his time well, the same principle could be applied once again to money-making. Motor magnate Henry Ford gave 500 copies of Bennett's book to his managers; another motor company president issued 18,000 copies, one to each employee.

The daily miracle

Philosophers have explained space. They have not explained time. It is the inexplicable raw material of everything. With it, all is possible,' without it, nothing. The supply of time is truly a daily miracle, an affair genuinely astonishing when one examines it. You wake up in the morning, and lo! your purse is magically filled with twenty-four hours of the unmanufactured tissue of the universe of your life! It is yours. It is the most precious of possessions. A highly singular commodity, showered upon you in a manner as singular as the commodity itself!

For remark! No one can take it from you. It is unstealable. And no one receives either more or less than you receive.

Talk about an ideal democracy! In the realm of time there is no aristocracy of wealth, and no aristocracy of intellect. Genius is never rewarded by even an extra hour a day. And there is no punishment. Waste your infinitely precious commodity as much as you will, and the supply will never be withheld from you. No mysterious power will say: 'This man is a fool, if not a knave. He does not deserve time; he shall be cut off at the meter.' It is more certain than government bonds, and payment of income is not affected by Sundays. Moreover, you cannot draw on the future. Impossible to get into debt! You can only waste the passing moment. You cannot waste tomorrow; it is kept for you. You cannot waste the next hour; it is kept for you.

I said the affair was a miracle. Is it not?

You have to live on this twenty-four-hours of daily time. Out of it you have to spin health, pleasure, money, content, respect, and the evolution of your immortal soul. Its right use, its most effective use, is a matter of the highest urgency and of the most thrilling actuality. All depends on that.

Arnold Bennett, *How To Live on Twenty-Four Hours* (1907)

The 'time is money' analogy is central to Bennett's argument. 'Why not concern yourself more with "How to live on a given income of time", instead of "How to live on a given income of money!" Money is far commoner than time,' he writes. 'When one reflects, one perceives that money is just about the commonest thing there is. The supply of time, though gloriously regular, is cruelly restricted.

'Which of us lives on twenty-four hours a day? And when I say "lives" I do not mean exists, nor "muddles through". Which of us is free from that uneasy feeling that the "great spending departments" of his daily life are not managed as they ought to be? Which of us is not saying to himself – which of us has not been saying to himself all his life: "I shall alter that when I have a little more time."

'We never shall have any more time. We have, and we have always had, all the time there is.'

The realization of this 'profound and neglected truth', as Bennett called it, should lead us to examine, in subsequent chapters, how time is wasted and to formulate some practical steps for improving our use of it.

KEY POINTS: TIME MANAGEMENT IN PERSPECTIVE

- Time is as mysterious as space. It is the dimension in which changes happen, balanced by relative continuities.
- Time can be measured with exceptional accuracy by clocks. Mechanical clocks have a profound influence on us. They make us even more time-conscious than our ancestors, although our increased life expectancy may make us less so in other respects.
- Clocks exert a discipline upon us. The Puritans in particular inculcated in Britain and the US a sense of the preciousness of time and the sinfulness of wasting it. Thrift, industry and punctuality go hand-in-hand.
- Not everyone operates on the 'time is money' analogy. Actually time is infinitely more valuable than money. It deserves to be treated with even greater respect.
- Only when you have perceived and assigned the right value to your time – more than gold or silver – are you

able to benefit from the practical suggestions in the remaining chapters of this book. A fresh realization of the intrinsic worth of your time engenders a burning desire in you to use it well.

> *It is not possible to hold the day.*
> *It is possible not to lose it.*
> From the face of a sundial (1695)

2

COMMON TIME PROBLEMS

Look in a mirror and you will see your biggest time waster. Until you come to grips with that reality, few if any of your personal time problems will be overcome.

Ironically the worst offenders are often those who seem to be working the hardest and longest. They may appear very busy but they are often not very effective. They do not always manage their time well.

This chapter aims to help you to identify some of your own and other people's major time problems and their causes. You may see elements of yourself in the five case studies to follow. They are like mirrors that are being held up for that purpose. If you do recognize yourself in one or two – or even all – of them, do not despair. Awareness and self-understanding are the first steps towards a complete cure. The whole of this book is intended to enable you to acquire good time management habits.

The case of the procrastinator

Robert Deal was potentially a good manager in many ways, especially in his relations with his staff. But they found his habit of procrastination infuriating. Even with minor matters he tended to postpone decisions until tomorrow – but tomorrow never comes. Two of his team members sometimes came out of his office complaining to each other, 'He has all the information we can afford to get and now is the time for decision but, once more, it's back to us for more work.' Mr. Deal was not incapable of decisiveness, however; he had just slipped into the habit of putting things off until tomorrow. This was especially noticeable when he was faced with unpleasant matters. Standards had been slipping in the office. A major personnel problem needed to be sorted out. Both issues were shelved until a more convenient time, but the time never seemed right. Reports, letters, and urgent requests piled up on his table. In the end this habit of procrastination proved his undoing. Typically, he delayed reading a letter warning about a forthcoming meeting, and went unprepared into the lion's den. The new chief executive fired him after the meeting.

Procrastination is often the vice of people who like to consider work rather than actually do it. As one of the characters in Jerome K. Jerome's *Three Men in a Boat* (1889) said, 'I like work; it fascinates me. I can sit and look at it for hours. I love to keep it by me: the idea of getting rid of it nearly breaks my heart.'

What is procrastination? How does it differ from, say, delaying a decision until more information is available? It can best be defined as putting off the doing of something that should be done – intentionally, habitually and reprehensibly.

If you suspect that you are prone to procrastination always ask yourself: '*Why* am I putting this off?' If you can see no good reason – and don't confuse reasons with excuses – then brace yourself and take action this day. 'Never leave that till tomorrow which you can do today,' wrote Benjamin Franklin.

Procrastination will mean that you are just about keeping

up with last week's business. By offloading today's work onto tomorrow you are simply storing up work for yourself. Tomorrow becomes the busiest day of the week.

Avoid delays! Resolve not to postpone what is ready to be done today. There is no time like the present. Wellington ascribed his unbroken victories as a military general to 'doing the day's business in the day'.

Be suspicious of yourself or others when deferment or delay is counselled. It may be just one more step on the road to dilatoriness. A wise person will indeed delay certain decisions or actions; there may genuinely be insufficient information or commitment. But he will never be in love with tomorrow, that most uncertain of all time's corridors.

You may not have heard of the English dramatist James Albery (1838–1889). As far as I know he achieved absolutely nothing – well, that's what can be assumed from his epitaph, anyway, and then history is not absolutely clear if he even wrote this himself or it was penned by another. A bit of further delving reveals that Albery was actually quite a busy man. However the ditty below perfectly sums up the life of a born procrastinator – if not him, does it describe you?

> He slept beneath the moon,
> He basked beneath the sun.
> He lived a life of going-to-do
> And died with nothing done.

Procrastination, which comes from the Latin word for 'tomorrow', is the world's number one time-waster. As one proverb says, it is the 'thief of time'. You must banish procrastination from your life if you want to become a better time manager. Be tough with yourself. Start now by doing something today that you have been putting off. It may be a small or large matter: an overdue apology; a confrontation with a low performer; a meeting with your boss; or an unpleasant task that you know you should tackle. The most difficult job of the day may not turn out to be as fearsome as you imagined.

The case of the poor delegator

The chairman, back from New Zealand that afternoon, suddenly summoned Tom Saunders, his chief executive, from his weekly management meeting. He pulled out the latest US paperback book called *How to Delegate* from his briefcase and gave it to Tom. 'That's your problem, Tom. You are carrying too much of the load of this company on your own shoulders. Read this by the end of next week and we'll have dinner and talk about it.'

Tom returned to the meeting fuming. 'As if I haven't got enough work,' he erupted. 'Now the chairman has given me a book to read. Where were we? Yes, I was asking you about the grade of oil I told you to use in the . . .'

'Hold on, Tom,' said Stephen Barnes, the finance director. 'I think the chairman has got a point. No one works harder than you but you can be over-attentive about details on the technical side. James is quite capable of handling them – it's his job – especially on the salary we are paying him! You do tend to interfere with those you have delegated responsibilities to, or at least it seems so to us. It's as if you don't quite trust us. And you waste a lot of your own valuable time checking administrative details and even doing a mass of routine work that others could do for you. If you did delegate more that would give you time to think about where this company is going in the next few years.'

'Everyone seems to be nodding in agreement with you' said Tom Saunders with a wry smile. 'All right, I'll read the book – if I have time over the weekend with all this to do.' He tapped his bulging briefcase. 'Now, about that oil . . .'

Delegation saves you time and develops team members. It does not save the organization's time, for someone else's time is being used. But it improves results by making fuller use of resources.

Failure to delegate eats your time. Again, always ask: 'Why am I not delegating?' Try to dig down to the real reason. Sometimes a manager is more comfortable doing the work of those he is managing: it is less challenging or threatening than the tasks he should be tackling himself.

Delegation implies good team members. Poor ones prefer to have their thinking done for them. They will always be pestering you for decisions or answers they could provide themselves. Never let them come to you with problems unless they bring their proposed solutions as well. Nine times out of ten you will be able to say, 'Fine, go and do it.' Eventually they will get the message and only come to you on the tenth occasion, when help from you is genuinely needed, for it will be something that only you can do.

Watch out for the phenomenon of upward delegation. Tom Saunders, the manager in the above case study whom I knew well, was especially prone to accepting jobs from his team members. These were tasks they ought to have done themselves. Usually they 'bounced' these chores onto Tom when they met him in the corridor or the lift. Being a willing workhorse and wanting to be helpful he rarely said no. But he certainly learnt his lesson after reading that book on delegation. I tried to get him to write up his case study for this book but he told me to do it myself!

Delegate as much as you can. Recognize also now that there is an art to delegation. It is simple but it is not easy. Chapter 9 explores the whole subject more fully. If you want to acquire the most important *strategic* time-saver, you must master the art of delegation.

CHECKLIST:
DO YOU NEED TO DELEGATE MORE?

	Yes	No
Are you frequently interrupted by members of your team with questions about their jobs or requests for advice and/or decisions?	☐	☐
Do you sometimes find yourself doing the job of one of your team members when he or she really ought to be doing it themselves?	☐	☐
Do you work longer hours than those of the employees that you manage?	☐	☐
Do you habitually take work home every night or at weekends?	☐	☐
Are you always rushed off your feet?	☐	☐
Do you set standards so high that only you can attain them?	☐	☐
Are you a constant 'checker-upper', keeping a close watch on the details of how your delegate is doing their job?	☐	☐
Do you have unfinished jobs piling up on your desk, or difficulty in meeting deadlines?	☐	☐
Does more of your time get spent in working on details rather than on strategic thinking, planning and other key leadership functions?	☐	☐
If so, do you work at details because you enjoy them, although someone else could look after them well enough?	☐	☐
Has anyone in the last year described you as being 'too conscientious' or 'rather too much of a perfectionist'?	☐	☐
Do you lack confidence in your staff's abilities and experience, so that you are afraid to risk giving them more decision making powers?	☐	☐

The case of the office mismanager

Henry Wilson shuffled through the papers piled high on his desk. 'This office looks like a jumble sale,' he sighed, briefly surveying the files, books, letters and unfinished contracts littering the floor and covering every available surface. 'Ah, here it is ... now where's my pen.' He sat down to write a reply to a letter but was interrupted by Bill Jenkins for ten minutes about some minor matter over the Nigerian contract. His secretary then brought in a pile of unopened mail for him to sort through but the telephone began to ring and Henry answered all nine calls himself. One wrong number, two wrong departments and another minor query from Bill, who still hadn't got his act together on the Nigerian order. Then it was coffee time, which took up another thirty or forty minutes, not least because Nancy his secretary wanted to tell him all about what the vet had said about her Dobermann Pinscher.

There was just time before lunch to deal with five telephone calls and to carry out another search among his papers for a missing telephone number. The afternoon was worse, with people dropping in without appointments or telephoning for a chat. By 5.30pm Henry had just about completed a short memo on stockpiling raw materials that was due to be sent last week. Just before he left for home he found five of that morning's letters, still unopened. One of them turned out to be a cancellation of the Nigerian project that everyone had assumed was going to happen – and Bill wasted an hour of his time about. Apparently the Nigerians had found a West German firm that could promise to deliver the equipment on schedule. They were weary of the delays they had experienced with Wilson's firm. 'The trouble is, Nancy,' said Henry Wilson as he stuffed the letters into his briefcase, 'there aren't enough hours in the day. God gave me only twenty-four hours a day – everyone else seems to have more.'

Henry Wilson is totally disorganized. He is snowed under with paperwork. He thinks he is busy but he isn't really. Interruptions in person or by telephone fragment his day, leaving him little time to achieve anything. When he goes home he often asks himself: 'What have I *done* today? What have I *achieved*?' The answer is usually nothing very much. Henry blames it all on not having enough hours in the day. But if he organized himself and his office better he would find that he has all the time he needs.

To deal effectively with paperwork you need a system. Chapter 7 sets out some advice on that score. Since the invention of the photocopier you are engaged in a battle for survival against the tide of papers that floods your office or rushes through the letter box. Only a ruthless policy of spending the minimum time possible on a piece of paper – handling it only once if possible – will save you from total ineffectiveness. The same applies to even newer technology such as emails and electronic memos.

Your secretary, PA or office manager, if you have one, should be competent enough to organize and run the administrative side of your office life. He or she should open the mail, sort it out according to some system of priority and screen your incoming calls and visitors to deflect the obvious time-wasters.

Answer the following questions honestly. If in doubt, ask someone such as your secretary or PA to check your answers – this may lead to some constructive dialogue.

CHECKLIST:
MANAGING TIME IN THE OFFICE?

	Yes	No
Are routine tasks in the office crowding out time I should be spending on urgent and important priorities?	☐	☐
Do I find myself constantly worrying about trivia?	☐	☐
Could I cut out some of the interruptions to my work each day?	☐	☐
Do I *like* interruptions, however irrelevant to my main concerns?	☐	☐
Are my desk and office in good order, with 'a place for everything and everything in its place'?	☐	☐
Does my secretary or PA act as a professional assistant, enabling the office to run more smoothly?	☐	☐

Muddle makes work and wastes time. Strive for good order in your office. Establish systems for dealing with the predictable and maintain them. Then you will find that you are free for the unpredictables – be they problems, crises or opportunities.

The case of the ineffective chairman

As an outstanding biologist Sally Hodson won promotion to Head of the Department of Microbiology at Jenner University, at the young age of thirty-two. Without any training in leadership she found herself trying to run a large department of sixteen academic staff, eight technical assistants, an administrative officer, secretaries and typists, as well as keeping up her own teaching and pursuing her important research.

Meetings of all kinds – research group, departmental,

faculty, university – seemed to fill the term, while meetings of another sort – conferences – occupied some of the vacations. At home there were yet more meetings: parents' associations, school governors, parish councils.

More often than not Sally found herself made chairman, usually because no one else wanted the job. Sally was in such a perpetual hurry that she didn't find time to prepare for meetings. Papers seldom arrived with the agenda – if there was one.

'Most meetings are a waste of time,' she told her husband. 'Half the time is spent discussing what the object of the meeting is. Usually it's a question of too many people – often the wrong ones at that – talking too much about too little.'

'Why don't you do something about it then?' suggested her husband. He was familiar with her litany of complaints about meetings.

'What *can* I do?' said Sally. 'People arrive late or leave early. As for the agenda, they jump around all over the place, never sticking to the subject. Trivial items, like the departmental notepaper, can take an hour. Next year's research budget is dismissed in five minutes. It's hopeless. Meetings drag on for two hours or more. And then no one ever seems to know what was agreed, let alone do anything about it.'

What do you think Sally Hodson could do about her meetings? She is caught in a time trap herself. But she is also wasting other people's time. She postpones meetings without consideration. Agendas are chopped and changed. There is inadequate preparation beforehand. Lack of control allows discussion to meander unchecked. Lastly, you notice that there are inadequate minutes, so that action after her meetings was usually confused.

Meetings of all kinds – formal committees to informal

meetings of two or three people in our room – involve others; therefore they are a potential time threat. This is because others can take up your time in wasteful ways if you are not careful, especially if they are nominally in control of the meeting. Always agree a time budget for a meeting of any sort and keep to it if possible.

Get into the habit of asking questions about meetings. Preferably you should do so *before* they happen. Here are seven key questions to help get you started:

- What would happen if we didn't have this meeting?
- Why are we meeting?
- What is the end product of this meeting?
- How long do we need for it?
- Who should be there?
- How can the meeting be best structured?
- When should it be held – is this the right time for it?

Unless you can satisfactorily answer these questions *do not hold the meeting*. Meetings are designed to save time. As chairman or member, you have a vital part to play to see that meetings begin and end on time, and accomplish their tasks in the most time-effective way.

The case of the undirected trainer

Liz Fellows worked in staff training in Midminster, one of the large clearing banks. A year after her start date she joined a group of about thirty trainers in a new group set up to provide a more comprehensive training service for managers and supervisors. She became increasingly frustrated by planning courses that were either cancelled or failed to attract enough participants. She complained to her manager: 'We are wasting a lot of time because we don't know what our aims and objectives are.

What are we trying to do? I feel as if I am working in the dark.'

'So do I,' said her manager. 'At head office they keep changing our priorities. This month it's our customer service campaign. The month before they were on about training for information technology. We have achieved some of our objectives, but no one can tell me what we are supposed to be doing at present. No one gives *me* a strategy or any policy guidelines, Liz, and so I can't help you.'

Liz Fellows went away in a thoughtful mood. That evening she told her husband, 'Now, I'm not even sure that I'm in the right job.'

With her enthusiasm dimmed and her morale low, Liz began to look elsewhere for another job. She went on to work as a saleswoman in a department store. 'At least I know the objective now,' she told her former manager when she met him in the street. 'Lucky you,' he replied, 'it's still the same confusion at the Midminster.'

It is difficult to manage your time effectively if you are not as clear as possible about your purpose, aims and objectives. Many organizations and work groups do not have a grasp of their 'core mission', let alone the more definite aims and objectives that should be channelling their sense of purpose in daily activity.

Within this framework you need a sense of priority – what needs to be done next. There are elaborate schemes in some textbooks on time management for what has come to be called 'prioritizing' – an ugly addition to the English language but nevertheless a useful one. But to arrive at your priority rating for anything you have to ask yourself two simple questions:

- How *important* is it?
- How *urgent* is it?

A priority may have different mixes of those two ingredients, which you can distinguish without too much difficulty.

EXERCISE 1: Reviewing your priorities

Review your priorities at present and list them – not more than five items – in a single column. Now grade them in order according to *importance*: A, B, C, D or E. On the other side grade them according to *urgency*: 1, 2, 3, 4 or 5.

Now re-list them according to their composite scores. There is no system for doing it, such as rating B4 higher than C1. You have to use your judgement.

Whether in personal or professional life, it pays to be clear about your aims and goals. That again sounds simple, but in practice it is difficult to obtain the necessary degree of clarity. Yet the fruit of clarity is that time management will become natural for you. You will have ceased to suffer from perhaps the most chronic time management problem of all – unclear objectives.

TIME MANAGEMENT – A PERSONAL CHALLENGE

Reading the five case studies in this chapter may have prompted you to identify symptoms that mark you out as a poor time manager. Once you have identified these areas for improvement you can begin to build a programme for change.

Improving your effectiveness in the use of time is like trying to become a better golf player. The perfect score is eighteen: a hole in one eighteen consecutive times. Obviously it is most improbable that anyone will ever achieve that score, but that doesn't stop keen golfers from endlessly trying to improve their game. In the process they may learn humility. As you strive to work economically and achieve more in your time, set yourself a similar aim. Perfection may elude you, but excellence is within your grasp.

Why not turn over a new leaf? It is never too late to make a fresh beginning. But you should be in no doubt that it is an exceptionally difficult task to become a good manager of your own and other people's time. Don't let the difficulty of it put you off, but regard it rather as a challenge.

The German dramatist Johann Goethe once remarked that writers begin books but readers finish them. If I could rephrase that, this book can offer the signposts and road maps of better time management but you must supply the motive power.

Pause for a moment and ask yourself: 'Do I really *want* to manage my time better? Am I prepared to pay the price of investing some time in reading and rereading these chapters, answering the checklists and making notes for action? Will I undertake to review my practical self-improvement pro-gramme every month for six months?'

'That is asking a lot,' you might say. Yes, but I can only repeat that time is our most precious resource. Nothing can be more rewarding at the end of our lives than a sense that we have spent more of it wisely than we have wasted.

On turning over a new leaf

The most important preliminary to the task of arranging one's life so that one may live fully and comfortably within one's daily budget of twenty-four hours is the calm realization of the extreme difficulty of the task, of the sacrifices and the endless effort which it demands. I cannot too strongly insist on this.

If you imagine that you will be able to achieve your ideal by ingeniously planning out a time-table with a pen on a piece of paper, you had better give up hope at once. If you are not prepared for discouragements and disillusions, if you will not be content with a small result for a big effort, then do not begin. Lie down again and resume the uneasy doze which you call your existence.

It is very sad, is it not, very depressing and sombre? And yet I think it is rather fine, too, this necessity for the tense bracing of the will before anything worth doing can be done. I rather like it myself. I feel it to be the chief thing that differentiates me from the cat by the fire.

'Well,' you say, 'assume that I am braced for the battle. Assume that I have carefully weighed and comprehended your ponderous remarks; how do I begin?' Dear sir, you simply begin. There is no magic method of beginning. If a man standing on the edge of a swimming-bath and wanting to jump into the cold water should ask you, 'How do I begin to jump?' you would merely reply, 'Just jump. Take hold of your nerves, and jump.'

As I have previously said, the chief beauty about the constant supply of time is that you cannot waste it in advance. The next year, the next day, the next hour are lying ready for you, as perfect, as unspoilt, as if you had never wasted or misapplied a single moment in all your career. Which fact is very gratifying and reassuring. You can turn over a new leaf every hour if you choose. Therefore no object is served in waiting till next week, or even until tomorrow. You may fancy that the water will be warmer next week. It won't. It will be colder.

Arnold Bennett, *How To Live on Twenty-Four Hours* (1907)

KEY POINTS: COMMON TIME PROBLEMS

- Never let procrastination root itself. It is a major time robber. Remember Benjamin Franklin's words: 'One today is worth two tomorrows.'
- Delegation does not save the organization's time, but it saves yours. The aim is to leave yourself free to do the work that only you can do. In practice that means delegating everything that can be delegated. But delegation is not abdication: you must establish and maintain a degree of control appropriate to the situation and the other person involved. In other words, there is an art to delegation that must be mastered.
- Efficiency in the office need not be soulless. If your offices, room or desk are in good order it is like having your ship cleared for action. You can begin to work effectively.
- Meetings are essential in any form of human enterprise. But they are potential time-wasters. The other person or persons present may not respect their own time as much as you have come to respect yours. It is then unlikely that they will mind wasting your time. Action is needed before, during and after a meeting to prevent this from happening. As a useful rule: always agree time limits at the outset of any meeting.
- You need to be clear about purpose, aims and objectives at work. The situation will then tell you what your priorities are in terms of importance and urgency. They are not necessarily the same thing.

You cannot kill time without injuring eternity.
Thoreau

3

DEVELOPING A PERSONAL
SENSE OF TIME

'If I were asked what one thing an executive could do that would really, and quickly, make him more effective, make him achieve more and make him enjoy what he's doing, I'd say: "Make sure you know where your time goes. Don't depend on memory, it's treacherous."'

Management guru Peter Drucker's words are an invitation to adopt something akin to a scientist's approach to time management. Put time under the microscope. You cannot *manage* time that is past. But you can examine how you managed it in an objective and realistic way.

The key suggestion in this chapter is that you should keep a Time Log, a record of how you are spending your time.

I warn you in advance, from personal experience, that you could be in for a considerable shock. Yet that very shock could jolt you into action. It is like an electric charge to start up the motor of your will. You may need the amazing revelation of how much time you are wasting to steel your resolve to manage time more effectively in the future.

You may say that you already know how you spend your time. Let me repeat Drucker's words: 'Don't depend on memory, it's treacherous.' The experiment is still worth trying, however certain you feel. You have nothing to lose. It may confirm your impressions, or it may make you think again, to your great benefit.

The end product is not a technique or – worse still – a complicated bureaucratic set of forms to fill in every week for the rest of your life. The exercise of making a Time Log should be a further step towards developing a personal sense of time: where it goes and where it should be going.

A personal sense of time

There is nothing which I wish more than that you should know, and which fewer people do know, than the true use and value of time. It is in everybody's mouth, but in few people's practice. Every fool, who scatters away his whole time in nothing, utters, however, some trite commonplace sentence, of which there are millions, to prove, at once, the value and the fleetness of time. The sundials all over Europe have some ingenious inscriptions to that effect; so that nobody squanders away their time without hearing and seeing daily how necessary it is to employ well, and how irrecoverable it is if lost.

Lord Chesterfield, *Letters to His Son* (1774)

Ask any ten managers or professional persons about the pressures on their time. At least nine will come up with the same sorry tales: long working hours, not meeting target dates and deadlines, fragmented days, excessive paperwork, and neglected families. A common refrain is that there aren't enough hours in the day. 'I just don't know where they go,' said one manager to me. He was one of the few who made the decision to find out.

KEEPING A TIME LOG

The principle of a time log or audit is to divide each day for the next week or two into fifteen-minute intervals. At the end of each hour you should record how the previous hour was spent.

You can use an ordinary large desk diary – one page to a day – for the purpose. Or you could use ruled sheets of paper or even type directly onto your computer. Find a format that you are comfortable with. You may find the symbols in the table overleaf useful.

You may, of course, want to amend or alter the list of prominent activities according to your trade or profession. For example, a teacher might include such headings as: Lesson/lecture preparation, marking, teaching, games and extracurricular activities.

It takes self-discipline to get started and keep going, but once you are into the swing of it, far less time is taken up by the exercise than you might imagine. In all it should occupy no more than five minutes a day.

Even as you do it you may find that your fifteen-minute coffee break usually runs to thirty minutes – you may, for instance, have to walk to a coffee machine and queue for your turn.

Look back at the end of each week. You may be surprised at what a comparatively small percentage of your time is actually used for the top-priority tasks on your list. Time for planning, anticipating contingencies, thinking about opportunities and recharging your batteries in various ways is often conspicuously missing, squeezed out by the day-to-day overloading or slippage from other more routine activities.

If so, it is a serious matter. For a manager's effectiveness is closely related to the use he or she makes of time. This

SYMBOLS FOR TIME LOG		
CODE AND ACTIVITY	DEFINITION, IF NECESSARY	NOTES
C Committees	Any prearranged group meeting with or without an agenda	
I Interviews	Any prearranged conversation, formal or informal, with a purpose	
D Discussion	Talking, not classified under C and I	
E Education	Participation in lectures, training courses, conferences and seminars	
F Figure work	Budgets, financial data and accounts	
P On the telephone		
S Dictating		
W Writing		
R Reading		
J Inspection	A personal tour of the work place, walking the job	
Q Travelling	For your work, and not doing other work listed above	
T Thinking		
O Others	Please specify what	

needs controlling, rather than the other way round, if he or she is to avoid constantly managing by crisis. In particular, achieving results through other people means that it is essential for the leader of the working group to manage his or her own time so tomorrow's problems are given time as well as today's decisions.

You may find that you had no idea how your time is really being spent. Memory isn't to be entirely trusted in this area because we tend to recall the productive hours of the day and to push into the background time wasted or not used to good effect. It is not unlike the old sundial inscription that reads: 'I record only the sunny hours.' The large pieces or small scraps of time taken up by matters of relatively minor importance are conveniently forgotten. These are the very items that a careful time audit should show up.

After keeping a log for three or four days, you may begin to notice opportunities for improvement. For example, you may discover that you are spending much more time than you thought on reading newspapers and trade journals or compiling routine reports. Could the latter be delegated? At the end of the two weeks, when the data is available, try to group your time use under key headings, such as:

SUMMARY OF TIME LOG DATA		
ACTIVITY	**HOURS SPENT**	**PER CENT OF TIME**
1. Committees		
2. Interviews		
3. Discussion		
4. Education		
5. Figure work		
6. On the telephone		
7. Dictating		
8. Writing		
9. Reading		
10. Inspection		
11. Travelling		
12. Thinking		
13. Others (specify)		

REVIEW AND REFLECT

After listing your findings in the above way you should carry out a rigorous review of how you are spending your time. Here is a series of questions that you should be able to answer:

- Do the time allocations reflect your priorities? Is the bulk of your time being spent on the key functions or core responsibilities of your job?
- What are the items that take up significant portions of your time and contribute nothing? What would happen if they weren't done at all?
- How much time each day is available for use at your own discretion, as opposed to being committed by other members of the organization? Could this time be consolidated into one period rather than in small isolated pieces?
- Could any of the work be done faster or simplified without adversely affecting other parts of the organization?
- Are you spending time on work that could be done to a satisfactory level by team members or your secretary? Look especially at constantly recurring problems, routine matters, or work to do with details.

Frequently the answers to these questions show that the tasks you consider to be most important in a management or professional sense are consuming the least number of hours.

To help correct the imbalance why not keep a daily activities log in terms of goals, objectives or results rather than activities? First you need to be clear about your goals and objectives – the subject of the next three chapters.

WHAT HAPPENS TO A MANAGER'S TIME?

In recent years many studies have been made, using the diary and/or observation methods, of management work. The following is the composite picture that emerges from that research.

Managers tend to work long hours, including paperwork done at home, business meetings and social events related to business. The hours often multiply in the higher echelons of a company, with those in well-defined jobs such as account-ants more likely to work shorter days. At work, managers are very busy. One first-line manager who was observed attended to over 300 separate things in a day, 'resting' for only one minute in an eight-hour period. Perhaps he knew he was being watched!

Work is fragmented into brief episodes, ranging from two to nine minutes. They do not follow each other in any particular order. Problems are dealt with by quick-fire decisions. No attempt is made to assess the priorities of issues by importance: everything is equally urgent. Interrup-tions are the order of the day. Some executives have as many as forty telephone calls and thirty visitors in the course of a single day. Paperwork, consultations, formal meetings, inspections jostle each other in untidy profusion.

Managers at all levels spend most of their time in their own departments. Senior executives are more likely to be in their offices or in other departments than on the shopfloor. Much Western practice has been shown to contrast with that of Japanese senior managers. When asked why he spent so much time on the shopfloor, the president of Toyota replied: 'We don't make cars in my office.' Most managerial communi-cations are oral, usually face-to-face in meetings. Contacts with colleagues increase with rank. Team members occupy between occupy between one-third and two-thirds of a manager's time, compared with superiors who spend only a fraction of that time with him or her.

Planning is a key leadership function, but the research shows that few managers are skilled in this area. Uninterrupted periods of time when planning is possible are rare in the average manager's diary. Less than 5 per cent of management time goes on planning.

Lastly, research confirms that we are not very good at estimating how much time we have spent on particular activities. For example, managers tend to overestimate the time taken up by production, paperwork, telephone calls, emails and thinking, and to underestimate the time that goes in meetings and discussions.

These studies raise the question: 'How much control can the manager have over his time?' One researcher wryly concluded: 'Even if the executives wanted to change their behaviour, they did not have much chance to do so. The content of their working day is determined only to a small extent by themselves and it is difficult to change it without making considerable alterations in the organizational structure of which they are part. Before we made our study, I always thought of a chief executive as the conductor of an orchestra standing aloof on his platform. Now I am in some respects inclined to see him as the puppet in a puppet show with hundreds of people pulling the strings and forcing him to act in one way or another.'

KEY POINTS: DEVELOPING A PERSONAL SENSE OF TIME

- Do not assume that you know how you are spending your time. For one or two weeks observe in detail and record how your time is spent.

- Analyse and consider the way that you have organized, planned, made, used and wasted your time in the five days. Then propose specific actions that you intend to take to improve your efficiency in this area. Compare how your time is actually spent against how it *ought* to be spent in the light of your job description and current aims and objectives.
- Studies of managers at work confirm that most of us mismanage our time. Yet time is our scarcest resource. Unless it is managed, nothing else can be managed.
- The result of reading this chapter and making a study of how you spend your time should be a development of your personal sense of time. That sense is essential, for it must influence you throughout the working day.

*Go, sir, gallop, and don't forget that the world was made in
    six days.*
You can ask me for anything you like, except time.

Napoleon

4

HOW TO IDENTIFY
LONG-TERM GOALS

All planning is thinking forward in time. What varies in plans is how far ahead they stretch and how precise they are. There is always a limit as to how far ahead it is feasible to plan at any given time. 'It is wise to look ahead,' Winston Churchill once said, 'but foolish to look further than you can see.' Beyond a certain prospect you are really dreaming rather than thinking.

Imagine you are walking through some hills. You can see objects very clearly in the *foreground* and soon come abreast of them. There is a middle ground, which is less close and also *far ground* – perhaps a range of higher hills. This analogy applies to life and work.

You will see that it is not possible to demarcate sharply between foreground and middle ground, or middle and far grounds. They all form part of a continuum that alters in shape as you advance.

Is the foreground – the time nearest to you – a matter of seconds, minutes, hours, days or weeks? It is impossible to be dogmatic, not least because your perception of what is or is not foreground in time is influenced by circumstantial factors. For example, a sick person's foreground might drop to a matter of minutes, just as mist or blinding rain can overtake you on the hills. You could be benighted – overtaken by darkness or night – so that your vision is reduced to a few metres ahead.

Despite these factors, the distinction between foreground, middle ground and far ground is valuable and you should train yourself to think and plan at all three ranges. Here, borrowing words from the military, I shall call those kinds of thinking *tactical*, *operational* and *strategic*.

This chapter aims to help you think strategically about your life and work. That presupposes an attempt on your part to look ahead, well beyond your present time commitments, to see if you can discern the shape of things to come. What is the geography you can make out on the horizon? You may want to select some features or areas – often by rejecting others – to which you will guide yourself. They can be called your *strategic goals*. Together they constitute your desired future.

LIFE PLANNING IN PERSPECTIVE

The present enthusiasm for life planning – setting strategic goals for one's life – has its origins in the US. It has become widespread in Britain and elsewhere through books on time management. You should be rather cautious about accepting the concept of life planning as a mental package.

The word *goal* comes from the world of sport. Originally it meant the terminal point of a race, such as a winning post. Now it covers both the area into which players in football and similar games attempt to drive the ball to win points and also the resulting score. In its more figurative or more general sense, a *goal* is the end towards which effort or ambition is directed.

People who love sport readily import analogies from sport into daily life. For example, 'That isn't cricket,' used to be a term of general disapproval in Britain. Now that the relish for competitive struggle and the value placed on winning the game have invaded cricket, as all other sports, the metaphor has somewhat lost its force.

Culturally, Americans have been shown to place even more value on winning than the British. They have been more inclined to see life as a competitive struggle, a game of winners and losers. The great thing is to be among the winners. As President Kennedy's father drummed into him: 'Coming second is coming *nowhere.*'

In such a culture the first questions to ask oneself in virtually any situation are: 'What is the game I am in? Where is the goal? How are the winners distinguished from the losers?' Goals in life tend to be competitive ones, such as to become president or to make a million dollars within ten years. Many strive to be president but only one secures the prize. Dollars are scarce and sought by all. If one person has a million, someone else will presumably have to make do with less. There are winners and losers in the marketplace as in politics.

Goal setting has proved remarkably successful. For example, when President Kennedy said that the US would put a man on the moon within ten years, it was like setting a goal for the nation. It was a competitive one too, for Russia could theoretically have beaten the US to it. That goal was admittedly achieved at the cost of a vast amount of human time and even vaster amounts of money. Was it all worth it? Could those resources have been spent more fruitfully on other terrestrial projects?

Actually, the Russians did not try to put a man on the moon before the Americans. Yet they were achieving other goals in space exploration; they were competing in the game.

Space now has a military use and is a factor in a new 'Great Game' of superpower relations. Sport and war are cousins.

The equivalent word for goal in the language of military theory and practice is *objective*. Literally it is the objective point towards which the advance of troops is directed. In its more general sense of being any point aimed at, the word objective has become one of several meaning *an end towards which effort is directed*.

The phrase *strategic goal* combines both the metaphors of war and sport. For *strategy* derives from the Greek words for a leader of an army. Strategy is the kind of thinking and planning appropriately done by a military general. It is the art of devising plans and employing stratagems towards achieving the general's ultimate objective of securing the enemy's surrender.

These sporting and military analogies – now hardly conspicuous as analogies, so common and so disguised are they in everyday speech – have much to be said in their favour. Goals are at least clear. By setting goals or objectives, vague aspirations are reduced into tangible and attainable forms. But the metaphors have more force in certain areas of life than in others. They apply especially to business enterprise in all its forms (see the following chapter). But they don't apply to whole sectors of your personal life. The analogies of life that liken it to playing a competitive game, fighting a war or running a business soon break down. They need to be supplemented by other analogies.

TO LIVE IS TO JOURNEY FORWARDS

Not everyone consciously thinks of his or her life as being like a journey, but the metaphor is deeply imbedded in Western culture. Here I should like to suggest some of the ways in which it is a helpful metaphor when looking ahead in your life.

Suppose you are making a journey that you have planned yourself. You can identify fairly clearly the place where you want to be tomorrow night. Let's call that your first *objective*. It's something tangible and immediately attainable. You can easily identify other objectives for other nights, culminating in the town or city where your journey ends. *End* has this convenient double meaning: end in time and end as aim or object.

For about three centuries the word *goal* has been used outside the context of sport to describe the destination of a difficult journey. It carries overtones of something attained only by prolonged effort and hardship. If you want to get to the top of Mount Everest or reach the South Pole you could accurately describe these places as goals. But when you get on the local train in the morning it is unlikely that you would call your destination a few stops down the line the *goal* of your journey. Though, of course, it might become a goal if the train breaks down and you have no other means of travel but to walk the next 20 miles.

The journey analogy is at least potentially free from the limiting overtones of competition and winners/losers. You can set objectives and goals for yourself that don't imply you are striving to be first. But like all analogies it fails to apply if pressed too far.

Strictly speaking there are no maps for the future. You can look up Mount Everest or the South Pole on the map and decide how to get there. But there are no 'places' that you can look up in a handbook of the future. In that respect, living is more like exploring an unknown country than following a route on a map.

But you can make general assumptions about the future. Experiencing life as relative continuity as well as rapid change, people act daily upon the probability that human society will remain more or less the same tomorrow as it is today. In the short term this allows you to act as if the future is predictable. For example, you might assume that the position of president of the US will be there in five years time. Therefore theoretically any senator or governor could plan to sit in the Oval Office of the White House. A whole host of careers – ready-made journeys – already exist. If you get on the right ladder or escalator in such careers you can most probably climb to a clearly discernible top.

Scaling these social or corporate heights step-by-step makes sense for some people, but not for others. It is less clear that strategic goals can be set in other areas of work, let alone the rest of one's life. Did Shakespeare set himself a strategic goal of becoming the world's most famous playwright and then plan his plays accordingly? It is highly improbable that he thought that way. But he may have dreamed of greatness when he was a boy. As the Spanish proverb says: 'If you build no castles in the air, you build no castles anywhere.'

You can also plan for part of your time but not for all of it. Some men do make a tangible goal – becoming the president of the US for example – the purpose of their lives. But this can become a straightjacket. When you have attained your goal, what do you do next? It is necessary to think in wider terms than a particular goal.

KNOW YOUR VALUES

Values are essentially what you think is worthwhile – that is, worth time – and deserving of effort. There is a reverse effect. If you spend time and energy on something or someone, you will value the object more than one that demands nothing from you. To some extent, by choosing an object and devoting ourselves to it, we create *value*.

In the context of time management, values potentially have a most important role to play. They are stars by which you can navigate. You will not succeed in touching them with your hands, but like the seafarer or desert traveller you choose them as guides and following them you reach your destination. Navigational skill is especially important at times when your future – for one reason or another – resembles more of an uncharted sea than the next stretch of a familiar river.

Values play this critical part in directing your course whether you are conscious of them or not. The first step towards better navigational skill is to become more aware of the values that are influencing your life choices now.

Is the price right? A tale about values

Peter Larking at first enjoyed his work as marketing director of a large cosmetics company. He liked the social life and the high salary he earned; he travelled all over the world staying in expensive hotels. But it was a burning ambition to head the multinational parent company that drove him to work all hours of the day and night. He spent the weekends thinking solely about business or talking to colleagues or customers on the telephone. At fifty-six years old – the year he gained a seat on the main board – his wife divorced him and he became ill with a second ulcer. The following year he had a coronary and on his doctor's advice had to give up his sole remaining 'pleasure' of mountain climbing. Just before his fifty-eighth birthday Peter was so busy managing a takeover bid – which if successful would almost certainly secure him the coveted job of chief executive – that he did not have time to visit his seriously ill eighteen-year-old son in hospital. The day after Peter got the top job his son died. 'Although I never had much time to spend with the boy,' he said to his secretary, 'he was the most important thing in the world to me.'

This cautionary tale is a reminder about knowing your values and keeping them in sight. Let other people question them if it serves to make you think more about them.

Know your values and adhere to them. But don't make the mistake of imposing them on others. In the words of pioneering US psychologist and philosopher William James: 'The first thing to learn in intercourse with others is non-interference with their own particular ways of being happy, provided that those ways are not assumed to interfere by violence with ours.'

A zest for living

If you want to enjoy one of the greatest luxuries in life, the luxury of having enough time, time to rest, time to think things through, time to get things done and know you have done them to the best of your ability, remember there is only one way. Take enough time to think and plan things in the order of their importance. Your life will take a new zest, you will add years to your life, and more life to your years. Let all your things have their places. Let each part of your business have its time.

Benjamin Franklin, US Founding Father and politician

Values can be expressed in the language of purpose, and statements of purpose can in turn be understood in terms of values. For example, if you make self-fulfilment your number one priority in life this may reveal that for you the value of the individual comes first. If the self-fulfilment of other individuals is what matters, well and good. If it is *your* self-fulfilment that counts, at the expense of others, then you may end up like Dr. Samuel Johnson's acquaintance – 'a lover of himself, without a rival'.

THE NATURE OF POLICY

Sometimes it is impossible to clearly identify a strategic goal. Then purposeful activity may be a matter of seeking to better your competitive position, a bit like a military general securing the commanding heights. You can improve your strategic capability. Even when you do not know precisely where you are going, some sort of forward movement is usually possible and may produce unexpected results. Remember, Columbus set out to find India but discovered America instead.

Alongside strategies and tactics of various kinds – the means you employ to achieve ends – must be placed *policies* and *routines*. What is their relation to time management? Routines will be discussed in the next chapter, so let us focus here upon policy.

A *policy* is essentially a *decision of principle*. It can help you to make choices when you face the need for them. You may have a policy of taking your holidays in the spring or autumn rather than in summer. This is not an invariable rule but a guideline. It saves you time because you don't have to think about when to take a holiday each year from scratch.

Policymaking is clearly important, whether it is done by an individual or by the leaders of a corporate body. To repeat the point, *it is not the same as a strategy*, although it may be related to it. Your policies are a body of principles that guide action.

Looking upon policies in this way prevents them from

becoming settled courses of action, definite procedures or routines. No one case is the same. The value of having policies, in the context of this book, stems from the fact that decision making is a time-consuming activity. If you can cut down time spent agonising over every problem by making some generic decisions instead, it could help to set you free.

A policy is not the same as a rule. A company may announce that its rule is not to give or receive bribes. Theoretically there is always the possibility of an exception but no exceptions are envisaged. A policy is a guide rather than a rule. It implies that the person applying it will use discretion and judgement.

Policies like rules should be absolutely clear, since their prime purpose is to prevent confusion and time wasting. A policy does not last forever. When in doubt it must be reviewed. When outdated or shown to be wrong it must be changed. If it is changed too often, then it fails to serve its purpose and actually causes confusion and wastes time. Order – counter order – disorder.

KEY POINTS: HOW TO IDENTIFY LONG-TERM GOALS

- The comparison of life to a journey is a powerful metaphor. Seeing your life in this way can be a positive help.
- Some journeys have objectives and routes; others are explorations into the unknown.
- Policy is not the same as strategy. You may be able to make progress without a strategy. When you encounter obstacles, problems or crises it is useful to have some clear policies as guides.
- A sense of purpose and a sense of direction can be developed. They come from the mental effort of trying to

identify at least some strategic goals and then pursuing them energetically. You can always modify or change them in the light of experience.

- Know your values, for they govern the direction and the manner in which you spend your time. Review them annually, setting aside some time to do so. Imagine them as the stars by which you are navigating the ship of your life.

- Don't interfere unnecessarily with the values of others. 'God knows well who are the best pilgrims.'

If you do not know where you are going you can take any road.

5

HOW TO MAKE
MIDDLE-TERM PLANS

Operational plans function in the middle ground of your life or your organization. In military terms, strategy is the concern of generals; tactics are the concern of colonels and below. Operational plans, coming in between, are the responsibility of divisional and brigade commanders.

What counts as the area of future time and activity subject to operational plans will vary widely. For you the middle ground may be the next three or four months, or a year or two at the most, while for a giant oil company or an international bank it could be much longer. Choose the length of time that suits you. Quarters of a year may suit you for progress review purposes, but not for forward planning. However you define the middle ground it will always merge into more distant time. For the purpose of this chapter I shall assume your middle ground is from one to twelve months.

As a principle, the further away in time things are, the less definite they are perceived to be. There are instruments such as telescopes that qualify this natural law in regard to space, but there is not yet a 'time machine' for the future. Operational planning concerns that stretch of the future that is neither immediately near to you, nor distant from you. Therefore, it will be fairly definite but not completely so.

Which should come first, strategic or operational planning of your use of time (along with the energy, talents and money available to you)? It doesn't really matter. Logically, of course, strategic thinking should be your priority. For if you do not know what point you are making for in the distant hills, it may be puzzling to know which route to take into the middle ground. But, leaving the analogy for a moment, engaging energetically in setting operational goals and objectives may lead on to the more distant future. In other words, a strategy may emerge from what is strictly speaking operational thinking. It is as if you can think either deductively or inductively about the future: ranging from the general to the particular, or the particular to the general. In some circumstances operational thinking may be the only option open to you. If so, start there.

TIME BUDGETING

Efficiency, it has been said, is doing things right, while effectiveness is doing the right things. But how do you know what are the *right* things to be doing with your time?

Clearly the first task is to sit back and ask yourself such questions as: 'What are my key goals and objectives in the next three months? What is it important for me to accomplish, progress or initiate? How should my life and work be different in a year's time from what they are now?'

Obviously the content of your answers will be unique to you. Here are some suggestions about the way to think clearly, so that the results of your operational planning meet the necessary criteria if they are to be implemented effectively.

Let us begin with the most difficult bit of all – sitting back. The object of moving your chair back is so that you can see a broader picture. Those preoccupied with day-to-day work often develop a form of tunnel vision. They cannot see the wood for the trees. For them the act of sitting back must be deliberate. It must be repeated time and time again, until it becomes second nature.

Imagine that your mind has two lenses, like a camera. The wide-angle lens allows you to see the wider picture of the middle ground, while your telescopic lens should enable you to focus upon a particular area of it in some detail.

You would see both a wider picture and further ahead if you could climb on to higher ground or be lifted up in a helicopter. Imagine yourself in a helicopter viewing the next six months. From this height the main feature should stand out in bold relief.

In the 1960s Shell identified this *helicopter vision* as a core ingredient of success in its senior managers (see table overleaf). Whether you are self-employed or work for an organization, you should develop this ability.

Reserve time for wide-angle planning. As the research studies in Chapter Two suggested, planning is often and easily squeezed out from an ineffective manager's day. Planning doesn't *demand* your attention. But don't neglect it. Invest time in thinking and planning ahead and it will pay you handsome dividends. Put some dates and times for planning down in your diary now.

It is often useful to go away for a day or two with your associates or team for this exercise. Being in different physical surroundings can have the psychological effect of distancing you from your everyday life, giving you a new perspective.

SHELL MANAGERS – VALUED QUALITIES	
QUALITY	**DEFINITION**
Imagination	The ability and drive to discern the various useful possibilities and alternatives that are inherent in a problem, but are not obvious to less perceptive observers.
Sense of reality	The extent to which: • An individual's interpretation of the action to be taken shows that full account has been taken of the realities of the situation. • An individual displays an almost instinctive feeling or intuition for the right course of action.
Power of analysis	The ability and drive to: • Transform, break down or reformulate an apparently complicated problem into workable terms. • Continue the analysis of the problem until all the relevant aspects have been thoroughly and critically examined.
Helicopter vision	The ability and drive to: • Look at problems from a higher vantage point with simultaneous attention to relevant details. • Place facts and problems within a broader context by immediately detecting relationships with systems of wider scope. • Shape one's work accordingly on the basis of a personal vision.

WHAT AN OPERATIONAL PLAN SHOULD DO FOR YOU

Essentially an operational plan should show you and others a limited but feasible number of goals and objectives, together with plans for achieving them.

In a given calendar period, assuming you are not starting from scratch, a group of objectives or plans will be in various stages of completion. It is like managing a portfolio of shares, each with its particular contribution and level of performance.

The plan proper should detail exactly what steps have to be taken to complete the task. When you have thought forwards, try thinking in reverse order too. This will help you to avoid leaving out essential steps.

A good plan will always answer the questions: Who? When? Where? How? What? and Why? In doubt or not, it is wise to check plans with someone else. You may be making some unconscious assumptions that another person will swiftly spot. Two heads are better than one.

What an operational plan will *not* do for you is make anything happen. It can be no more than an architect's blueprint. If you are only an architect and not a builder, nothing will happen.

On the other hand, a good operational plan will save you time – lots of it. There are research studies to confirm what common sense tells you: the more time spent planning a project, the less total time is required for it.

Imagine two groups tackling the same common task. Group A skimps on planning: the leader is action-centred in the wrong sense of that phrase – he regards thinking as a waste of time. As a consequence, Group A takes a long time to complete the task. Nobody in that group is clear on the objective; alternative courses of action have not been explored.

By contrast, Group B takes adequate time to plan. The objective is made clear and definite; time limits and other boundaries are clarified. The optimum course of action or solution is chosen from a list of feasible options. There may even have been a brainstorming session to help generate creative ideas. Everyone feels committed. The job gets done faster.

PLANNING/IMPLEMENTATION RATIO

GROUP A

PLANNING	IMPLEMENTATION

GROUP B

PLANNING	IMPLEMENTATION

A casual observer in the planning phase may have given marks to the leader of Group A for decisiveness. But looking at the exercise overall it is clear who made the better decisions.

The principle that 'planning saves time' applies at the strategic, operational and tactical levels. Always work on the key principle that: 'Every moment spent planning saves three or four in execution.'

CHARACTERISTICS OF GOALS AND OBJECTIVES

To summarize earlier points: goals and objectives are words drawn from the sports field and the battlefield respectively.

They should be definite in the sense of being well defined. Objectives are tangible and near at hand; the archery target is a good analogy here. Goals may imply more distance or greater difficulty.

Assuming that a page or two ago you identified at least one objective for the next six months of your life or work, now check it against the following criteria:

CHECKLIST – HALLMARKS OF GOOD OBJECTIVES

CLEAR	☐	REALISTIC	☐
SPECIFIC	☐	CHALLENGING	☐
MEASURABLE	☐	AGREED	☐
ATTAINABLE	☐	CONSISTENT	☐
WRITTEN	☐	WORTHWHILE	☐
TIME-BOUNDED	☐	PARTICIPATIVE	☐

You may not have ticked all the boxes. This may not matter. For example, some objectives can only be measured by judgement rather than by quantitative methods and you may hesitate to tick MEASURABLE. If you are setting a personal objective – such as to compete in a marathon and complete the course within the top half of the field – then PARTICI-PATIVE may not be relevant. There should, however, be a lot of ticks, thereby illustrating that you are meeting many criteria. Otherwise your objective is too vague and you are dealing in hopes rather than plans.

TIME NORMS FOR ROUTINE ACTIVITIES

When thinking ahead about our lives or work the centrepiece will tend to be formed of goals and objectives. For example, a manager may want a promotion or to buy a new house.

His corporate objectives in the next six months may include the successful launch of a new product in the North-East. But in the background are the continuing activities that cannot really be described as goal-seeking. They are usually lumped under the heading of *routine*.

From the French word *route* – a gravelled way – routine means an established course of procedure, something you do habitually and regularly. It is like the road leading to your house: you know the road so well that you do not have to think about such things as direction as you drive down it. Therefore it is a more routine and potentially less interesting road than the unknown road you explore on holiday.

Simply because they are so commonplace, routines can easily be overlooked in time management. As they become more mechanical, inflexible and uninspired, routines may also become more time consuming. If so, they cease to be worth the time allowed for them. Moreover, being more-or-less habitual, they tend to escape close scrutiny.

Before your next operational planning session, try to identify some of these established and recurring activities, using the table below to chart them. It may be worth holding them up to the touchstones of purpose and aims, goals and objectives. You or your staff can prepare for this review by keeping track of how much time these tasks normally take. If necessary, break them down into measurable parts using work-study methods. Then assign a realistic norm – the amount of time you think the task should take. This approach should:

- Highlight any routine activity that seems to be consuming a disproportionate amount of time. If it is something you are doing yourself and you have others working under you, consider delegating some or all of it. You may want to question why it is being done at all.

- Assist in replanning your work. Any major deviation from the time norm will suggest a need for time management action.
- Prevent the application of Parkinson's Law – that work expands to fill the time available for it.

TIME NORMS	
ACTIVITY OR PROCEDURE	**TIME NORM**

Time norms for routine tasks can be seen as challenges. Indeed by setting time norms for these regular courses or procedures, you are beginning to turn them into an objective.

You can build on this idea by introducing success criteria to inoculate against the deadening effects of routine: mechanical, uninspired and inflexible driving down well-travelled roads.

THE QUARTERLY REVIEW

At three, four or six monthly intervals – whichever suits your situation – you should carry out a progress review. Look upon it as a learning experience, for you can only master the skills of time planning by practice. But practice without subsequent reflection matching it against theory or principles is useless.

Look in particular at objectives you failed to achieve in the period under review. What went wrong? There are four possible causes listed in the table below. Avoid blaming external circumstances too much: it can become a habit.

DIAGNOSING CAUSES OF LIMITED SUCCESS	
Circumstances beyond your control	Could you not have foreseen these circumstances four or six months ago? What indicators did you ignore?
Circumstances within your control	Were there factors within your control, such as recruiting enough staff, which you ignored or handled badly? Did the failure lie within your powers as an implementer rather than planner?
Insufficient motivation	Did you write down four or six months ago some objectives that you had no real intention of completing? Goals are demanding: did the difficulty involved reveal your lack of motivation?
Insufficient skill in setting objectives	Review the actual goals or objectives against the twelve 'Hallmarks of good objectives' criteria on page 55. Did the lack of a deadline, for example, explain why the job was not done on time?

People often rationalize failures due to their own shortcomings by blaming factors that they assume, claim or pretend were outside their dominion.

If you have been thinking strategically during the period under review you may well have abandoned or altered an objective for a perfectly good reason. Perhaps a more strategically important opportunity suddenly opened up, or a genuine obstacle in your path caused you to alter course. Planning should always have contingency provisions. Uncommitted resources, if only some of your own time, should be kept in reserve. Unexpected opportunities and problems, even crises, are part and parcel of life. A wise manager plans with such pleasant or unpleasant contingencies in mind. As one general put it: 'A plan is a very good basis for changing your mind.'

KEY POINTS: HOW TO MAKE MIDDLE-TERM PLANS

- Develop your *helicopter vision* – the skill of taking a broader and longer look at the work you are doing. Set it in strategic context and identify key operational goals and objectives.
- A plan gives you something to work on. But it is only half the battle. The other half is to implement it. Remember that planning saves time by cutting down time needed for execution.
- Goals and objectives should not be vague. There is an art in setting them for yourself or others. Like silver, the genuine article should bear certain hallmarks, such as being specific, measurable and subject to a deadline.
- You can only learn how to set objectives by setting them and by reviewing performance afterwards. In the case of

limited success, thinking backwards after the expiry date
should enable you to identify which of the four causes of
limited success on page 58 led to failure. Don't make the
same mistake three times.

- Stay flexible, especially over the means by which you plan
  to achieve the objective. Change objectives more slowly,
  and then only if a better opportunity arises or external
  factors really compel you to do so.

*If you want something to happen you must make time and
space for it.*

6

PLANNING THE DAY

'After all your years of experience in management, do you have a golden rule for managers?' This question was put to management guru Peter Drucker at a London conference.

'I have no experience in management but I have seen a lot of managers as an outsider,' replied Drucker. 'One golden rule is to ask yourself if you know what you are being paid to do – and do not believe the answer is work. What are the two or three things that if you really perform will make a difference? If you do this, the rest easily takes care of itself.'

Strategical and operational planning, the subject of the last two chapters, should have provided you with an answer to Drucker's question. Within a framework of clear, ordered and truthful thinking about yourself and your future you should now be able to get down to the tactical level of 'telescopic lens' focus and planning with real confidence.

This chapter is about how to plan effectively the time that is immediately available to you – today. A day is a natural unit of time. As yesterday is gone and tomorrow is yet to be, it follows that today must take centre stage in tactical time management.

ATTITUDES TO TIME

Before plunging into the practicalities of daily time management it is worth asking yourself each morning: 'Do I intend
to live in the present today?' For it is actually sometimes
quite difficult to live fully in the present. Sometimes, for
what seems a perfectly good reason, yesterday or tomorrow
attracts us far more than today.

Here is another possible issue for your fundamental thinking programme. What is your philosophy about the value of
today, as compared to tomorrow or yesterday? Does your
philosophy help you to give yourself to the demands and
joys, disappointments and opportunities, of today?

Sometimes people resolve the matter by saying that today
alone is real. But you cannot be sure of that. In some sense
yesterday is still real and tomorrow may be as well. If you
define reality as what you can see, touch or experience in the
present, you reduce its meaning. Reality is partly a human
value judgement. If you value tomorrow more than today it
may indeed be more real to you.

Escapism is consciously or unconsciously diverting your
mind to purely imaginary activity or entertainment to escape
from the realities or routines of today. You can also escape
from today by living imaginatively in the past or the future.
Of course escapism in itself is not necessarily good or bad:
we are all escapists on occasion, not least because our minds
need refreshment and recreation as well as our bodies. But
habitual escapism is another matter: it militates against any
form of managing your time well.

Philosophy and religion are partly about freeing people to
live today. Faith can deliver from care or anxiety about
tomorrow and regret or guilt about yesterday. It can engineer
in us a valuable attitude to the past, based on gratitude. So

we can remember the past without reliving it each day. There can grow in us an attitude of hope towards the future that is not quite the same as optimism.

Experiencing that ideal of living 100 per cent in the present minute, incidentally, is sometimes literally marvellous. To be totally absorbed in what you are doing is a mystical experience in its own right.

Most of us fall short of this ideal. This is necessarily so because today is framed by yesterday and tomorrow, just as this minute or hour is framed – given meaning – by its context of the time before and after. It is human for us 'to look behind and before, and pine for what is not'. The problem is one of balance more than anything else. The previous two chapters have been concerned with looking ahead to the far ground and middle ground of the probable future. Both individuals in their working lives and corporate enterprises need to imagine and to plan realistically where and what they want to be in, say, five years' time, and then again over shorter periods such as the next three months. Part of today's meaning or significance must come from its place in that scheme of things. But today has its own autonomy.

I see now that today is both the aftermath of all my yesterdays and the prelude to all my tomorrows. It is the time when, if I choose to do so, I can reflect and review the past, my own or the past in some more general sense. It is the time when I can think forwards and try to identify the stars by which to direct my course in the future. But it is also a day in its own right, with a unique set of people, demands, duties, opportunities, hopes and fears. Some of these may link up with the future and some may not. It is part of the fun that I have no means of telling, except perhaps the occasional flash of insight or the promptings of intuition. Only at some future date, when I look back, will I be able to see what was significant or not.

From these reflections, if you agree with the conclusion, you can see our attention should be gently and firmly directed onto today. As for the future, it still awaits creation. Today's work well done remains your best preparation for it. And to do work that builds on yesterday's work and prepares for tomorrow you need to budget your time for each day with care.

As a personal policy, I suggest that thinking directly about the future or the past should occupy no more than 10 per cent of your time a day. Days that you have set aside for planning or review will be obvious exceptions to this rule.

BEGINNING WITH THE YEAR'S DIARY

Diaries are essential tools for time planners. There's something inherently pleasurable about the gift of next year's diary: all those empty pages, the promise of another year of life.

The shape or form of your diary is mostly a matter of personal choice. Many people prefer a combination of a large desk diary – a page-per-day that lives in the office and is used also by their secretary, PA or team members – together with a personal pocket diary. New technology in the form of computers and personal digital assistants (PDAs) has also allowed for electronic versions of the paper diary – ones that can be accessed by invited members with facilities for personal or private information.

It is essential, of course, to keep these synchronized, otherwise you will be accepting invitations to meetings when it appears that you are free for something else.

Various commercial time management diaries are now on the market. Some offer an eighteen-month or two-year 'time planner' chart, which is useful if you book that far ahead. It is wise to have a policy as to how far ahead you are prepared to commit yourself. As a principle, keep your options open as long as possible. Don't commit your time too far ahead unless you are sure it's right for you to do so. Committing time in this way, like writing cheques, is easily done, but can be painful when the day of settlement arrives.

Personally, I still find a Filofax-style diary system that I can assemble myself most useful. In a loose-leaf leather notebook you can clip in the diary of your choice plus a selection of other useful pages. You can also keep some notes on your key aims and objectives under the same cover as your calendar diary: a valuable reminder that they belong together.

Planning the day

He who every morning plans the transaction of the day and follows out that plan carries a thread that will guide him through the labyrinth of the most busy life. The orderly arrangement of his time is like a ray of light which darts itself through all his occupations. But where no plan is laid, where the disposal of time is surrendered merely to the chance of incidents, chaos will soon reign.

Victor Hugo, French writer

Having obtained or formatted next year's diary, block out holidays, family dates, and non-work events, such as meetings of local committees or councils of which you are a member. These are your *committed times*. Make sure you transfer all your work commitments into the new diary as well. Add in any important deadlines by which activities have to be completed.

Suddenly, the blank year begins to look rather full. There

is still plenty of uncommitted time, however, and managing that time well must be your principal priority.

THE DAILY LIST

It is an essential discipline to compile a programme for the day. Make out a fresh list of what you have on and also what you want to achieve in the free time available. Don't rely solely on your diary entries as it is unlikely that they will cover the whole of your day. You should add them into your daily list instead. Later, with experience, you may be able to make the list mentally, using your diary as a memory aid or using a written or typed list only on complicated days.

Set time limits for all tasks. Get into the way of always estimating the amount of time required to do each job, such as conducting an interview or writing a report. Check afterwards to see if your estimate was realistic.

Then establish your priorities. A priority is composed of two elements in various mixtures: *urgency* and *importance*. Repairing that punctured tyre on your car is urgent but it is not important. It is important that you begin to think about next year's marketing strategy but it is not urgent. But it is both urgent and important that you convince the chief executive about new sales campaigns at your 4.30pm meeting today.

Some tasks that lack importance and urgency may be worth achieving first. The time–benefit ratio can be a good guide here. If the benefit is substantial and the time taken is small, do it. For example, before you can settle down to an important item, such as composing a letter to your chief client with a proposition, there may be a couple of minor tasks you can delegate. Your use of a few minutes to assign or delegate these tasks gives more notice to relevant team members and makes more sense.

Some people find it useful to have a system of letters, numbers, colours or stars to make the various orders of priority. A letter system – A, B, C and so on – might include:

A   MUST be done today
B   SHOULD be done today
C   MIGHT be done today

It may be that you do not reach the bottom of your A and B lists but do not let that bother you. If you have worked according to your sense of priorities, you will have done the important jobs, and that is what managing your time at work is about.

Planning your day should not be done in a few minutes on the back of an envelope. Budget a reasonable time for your daily planning. Some people like to do it at the beginning of the day's work. Others prefer to plan their day the night before. This has the advantage that you can sleep on it. Sometimes after a night's rest other points for your list will occur to you or you may alter your priorities. Your subconscious mind will often suggest these alterations like a computer doing its work for you.

Check through your planned day to see if there are any gaps, any pieces of marginal time that can be filled or put to good use. As the German philosopher Friedrich Nietzsche said: 'When one has much to put into them, a day has a hundred pockets.' You are more likely to fill the spare pockets if you identify them in advance and allocate some tasks – such as writing a letter or making a telephone call – to them.

One word of caution: if you find yourself transferring an item on your list from one day to another it may be a sign that you are procrastinating. Scrutinize the item and your list carefully to ensure that this is not the case.

Remember also to remain flexible. Someone – such as a family member or important customer – may put in a claim on your time and they may deserve a higher priority than the next item on your list.

What matters most now? That is the question you should be asking yourself constantly throughout the day. The answers must be related to constantly changing circumstances and the needs of the minute yet they must not be mutually self-defeating in the longer term. It is essentially a series of value judgements, requiring from you a rare measure of mental discipline in the service of an unerring sense of time.

Valuable advice

Charles M. Schwab, who transformed Bethlehem Steel Company into the largest independent steel producer in the world, once issued a challenge over the dinner table to a management consultant named Ivy Lee: 'Show me a way to get more things done with my time and I'll pay you any fee within reason.' Lee handed him a pad of blank paper. 'Each evening write down the things you have to do tomorrow,' he said, 'and number them in order of importance. First thing in the morning start working on item one and continue with it until you have finished. Then start on item two ... then the same with three ... then four. Don't be worried if you haven't finished them all. If you can't do it by this method you can't do it by any other. Use this system every day.'

Shortly afterwards Schwab sent Lee a cheque for $25,000. He said later that it was the most profitable lesson he had ever learnt in his business career.

This practice of spending the last few minutes of each working day preparing your list for the next morning has much to commend it. Successful managers have mentioned this more frequently than anything else as an aid to effective time management. If postponed until the morning, list preparation is often done in a hurried or perfunctory way as other activities begin to press on your time. The urgent items then tend to dominate, completely eclipsing the important items that should be in places number one, two or three.

If you find that your daily planning is not working very well, ask yourself first: 'Am I at least achieving my highest priorities?' If the answer is 'No' or 'Doubtful – some of the time only', you should work through the following checklist of questions:

- Are you trying to accomplish too much in a day?
- Did some tasks not get done because you were not ready at that time to do them?
- Was the item or task clearly formulated?
- Do you find it difficult to make decisions?
- Did you have all the available information?
- Had you neglected to plan sufficiently for the day because you were feeling under pressure?
- Did you abandon the task because it was too difficult or too boring?
- Was lack of self-confidence at the root of the failure?

A review of this kind can establish whether or not your time budget was realistic in the first place. If it was realistic then the problem lies in the area of execution.

The most common reason given to me by managers for failing to accomplish what they set out to do is summarized in one word – interruptions. There are good and not-so-good interruptions. Sometimes, as for a doctor on call in the middle of the night, an interruption is merely a summons to do the job we are paid for. Other potential interruptions are more like contrary winds pushing us off course. To counter them you must learn to use one of the shortest and most time-saving words in the English language – 'No'.

LEARN TO SAY NO

Effectiveness at work depends upon knowing what *not* to do. Over-commitment is a sure road to failure. It can lead to a breakdown in your health.

Sue Townsend, author of the bestselling 'Adrian Mole' books, had a heart attack at the age of forty. 'I had become something of a workaholic without realizing it,' she confessed. 'I did everything anyone asked me to do. I suppose it's a form of insecurity but I've never been able to say "No". Since my heart attack I have improved and I usually insist on sleeping on any proposal, often before turning it down.'

You may find it hard to refuse someone's request for your time. Possibly you feel that the other person will think less of you for doing so. Learn to decline with tact and firmness.

Don't misunderstand me; I'm not counselling you against helping people. I'm talking about the times when you say 'Yes', when in your heart you know it should have been 'No'. For you could have put that time to better use.

When you say no, if possible say it promptly. Thus you will avoid raising false hopes only to be dashed later. Such vague phrases as 'Let me think about it' or 'I don't know' do breed expectancy. Of course, if you are in genuine doubt, by all means play for time. Ask for more information, perhaps in the form of a written request with background data.

Remember that you do have the right to say no. Although it is normally courteous to give a reason, even an invented one, you do not have to excuse yourself every time you turn down a request. Politeness is never out of place. Be sensitive as well; you may think you have more important matters to attend to but the other person may have different ideas. What is important and what is not depends to some extent upon where you are sitting.

THE TIME FANATIC

You are now growing more enthusiastic and becoming more skilled in daily time management. That puts you at risk of becoming a time fanatic. The author Arnold Bennett warned his readers against 'the terrible danger of becoming that most odious and least supportable of persons – a prig'. He defined a prig as 'a tedious individual who, having made a discovery, is so impressed by his discovery that he is capable of being gravely displeased because the entire world is not also impressed by it'.

Therefore, when you set out on the enterprise of using all your time, it is just as well to remind yourself that your own time, and not other people's time, is the material with which you have to work. The world turned on its axis before you began to budget your time and will continue to roll on regardless of what you do with your day. Refrain from talking too much about your new enthusiasm or overacting the part of time manager. Avoid telling your wife, children, boss or team members how much time they are wasting each day. You will ultimately find that managing your own time is all you can do.

Another danger is being tied to your programme. A daily list is a good servant but a bad master. Your daily to-do list of priorities should be respected but not canonized into holy writ. It is a tool to be used, not an idol for worship. 'To treat one's programme with exactly the right amount of deference, to live with not too much and not too little elasticity is scarcely the simple affair it may appear to the inexperienced,' concluded Arnold Bennett.

The to-do list can become like a tyrant in people's lives, be they chief executives or those trying to run a house. The following passage, by Cambridge historian Dr. Jonathan Steinberg, should help to inoculate you against the danger of becoming a complete time management fanatic:

> The unexpected caller, pleasant or unpleasant, disturbs the pattern of your time. That time is already allotted. Hence there is no time to help somebody who needs it, to relax and enjoy a chat on the street.
>
> Enjoyment is always for *after* when all the jobs with deadlines, the letters to be answered, the calls to be made, have been despatched. But that time never comes. There are always more letters, deadlines, jobs and so life gets postponed until an indefinite *after* – until it is too late. A hamster on a treadmill has about the same sort of freedom.

Using time effectively should always be your ideal but it should never become an obsession. If your values are right it never will. Remember always the end for which time is being managed. If a more important end appears, be flexible. One of the aims of daily time management is precisely to be free in this way: to have time to spare for the unexpected. That entails doing what needs to be done in the most economical way. When you are not fishing, mend your nets.

KEY POINTS: PLANNING THE DAY

- Tactical planning focuses upon the immediate time available to you, which is measured out in days.
- Check your attitude to the present, for without concentrating on today – at the expense of thinking about yesterday or tomorrow – you will achieve nothing.
- Make out a list of what you want to do each day – a shopping list of items arranged or marked in some order of priority. Do it the evening before so that you can sleep on it.
- Review each day briefly, identifying the successes, analysing the reasons for the failures. Avoid making excuses for yourself to yourself; dig down for the real reasons.
- Learn to say 'No', otherwise you will merely become a servant to the priorities of others.
- It is not easy to become efficient without being odious. Your practice of time management should enable you to contribute more to society and to others, not act as their judge.
- Do not become a slave to your planned daily programme. The aim is to free yourself from time pressures in order to work and to live more rewardingly. There's always time for important things. If something is important, you'll make time for it. Try always to enjoy whatever you are doing, and don't waste time regretting what you don't make time to do.

It's not enough to be busy. The question is: What are you busy about?

Henry Thoreau, US writer and activist

7

MAKING BEST USE OF YOUR BEST TIME

The quality of time matters more than the quantity of time. Therefore what could be called quality control of your time should be a matter of absorbing interest to you. The chief principle here is to make the *best use* of your *best time*.

The first aim of this chapter is to make you aware of what your best or naturally high-quality time is, so that you can employ it for high-quality work. As work of this nature will almost certainly involve thinking in some form or another, the second aim of the chapter is to remind you of how to use your brain effectively.

You may feel that you know yourself pretty well. But research suggests, rather surprisingly, that most managers either cannot identify the hours when they are naturally more mentally active or do not plan their time with this factor in mind. Therefore high-quality time is often partially wasted on low-quality activities.

Finding the best time

Mary Stannard's husband was made redundant by a US pharmaceutical company where he had been a sales manager. Nothing suitable came up in the way of a job and after a year he and Mary decided to invest the redundancy money by buying a corner shop in Farnham. Some time earlier, Mary had discovered that she had a real interest in and talent for becoming a journalist but she had left her secretarial job when the children were born and never followed it up. Now Mary resolved that after she had sent the children to school, done the housework, helped her husband in the shop, filled in the daily accounts and looked after her ageing mother who lived nearby, she would really get down to some writing. After all, they now needed some extra income. 'I'll help,' volunteered her husband. 'I'll put the children to bed and cook supper every night.' But by 5pm when Mary finally sat down at her computer, she was too tired even to think. What should she do?

WHAT IS YOUR BEST TIME?

Essentially it is the time when you do your best work. You can discover it by the process of experiment. Maybe for you it's early in the morning, perhaps in the afternoon or late in the evening. Winston Churchill used to work best late at night and in the early hours of the morning. He did not get up before breakfast; instead he stayed in bed most of the morning reading papers, dictating letters or seeing people.

Some people concentrate or function best around lunch time or later in the afternoon, but the main two camps seem to be 'larks' – those who function best in the morning – and 'night owls' – those who do better during the night hours. Either way you need to develop a strategy based upon using your prime time for creative thinking or strategically signifi-cant pieces of work.

Acting on your best time

A friend of aspiring journalist Mary Stannard, who had read about the principle of making best use of your best time, suggested that Mary should postpone such chores as housework and bookkeeping to the afternoon and make an arrangement with her husband to only help in the shop before lunch and at closing time – the shop's busiest hours. By getting up for an hour before breakfast, Mary found her solution. She could write for two hours between 9.30am and 11.30am. 'Actually I can do five hours' work in those two hours,' she told her husband after the first week. A year later she had become a part-time reporter for the local newspaper and a regular contributor to various national journals.

Research shows that many people think best early in the morning – why is this? Consider the relation between mental and physical fatigue. A manager who has completed a long, hard day's work arrives home suffering from mental fatigue. His eyes and facial muscles feel tired; he is irritable; he avoids more mental work and finds it hard to make decisions. If he does have to make decisions while in this state, the quality will be suspect. He wants to relax, yet thoughts keep crowding in on his mind. The remedy for such mental fatigue is not more work but recreation, outdoor exercise or any activity that holds his interest without making demands on his brain.

Some years ago an experiment was carried out to measure mental fatigue. A man was given a number of arithmetical problems consisting of the mental multiplication of two sets of four-figure numbers. Starting at 11am he continued without a break until 11pm. He completed sixty-seven sums. The time taken for each problem increased from five minutes for the first problem to about ten minutes for the last one. That was due, quite understandably, to fatigue.

A different man was set the same test starting at 11pm after a hard day at work. For the first twenty problems he did as well as the other, taking about an hour and a half. Then he went to pieces, taking up to twenty minutes for a single problem. Clearly an additional factor had come into play.

For humans, there seems to be a natural rhythm of getting up some time after dawn and going to bed some time after sunset. This rhythm is extremely hard to break; even after long spells of working the nightshift and sleeping during the day, a human will show proneness to fatigue in approximately the following proportions:

Even when you have been awake all night, your natural human bodyclock is designed to send you a new rush of energy just as dawn breaks. The pattern and insistence of this rhythm varies with individual temperaments, with habit and with climate. But it affects most of us so strongly that in normal conditions it is a good policy to programme creative or demanding work when your energy level is rising – usually before or after breakfast. For most of us the morning is the time for hard or focused work. 'Interesting' work – certain meetings or social events – can then be put in your off-peak time to give yourself some extra stimulation.

Remember it is more time-economical to remedy fatigue before it becomes acute. The less fatigue, the shorter the rest needed to restore you to full efficiency. It is better to part-exchange your car for a good price rather than use it until it's only fit for the scrap heap. Breaks have an essential part to play here. Having an hour off for lunch is obviously important, especially as it gives you the chance to get outdoors or at least away from your desk, computer screen or usual workspace. The best position for shorter breaks is just after the peak of morning and afternoon work – say at 11am and again at 4pm. We tend to work harder, as if putting on a spurt, just before and sometimes just after a break. Anticipation plays a part here. Also the value of the break depends upon its length and the way in which it is spent. If the break is too long it will waste time, or it may do positive harm by loss of mental momentum – the equivalent to an athlete's muscles hardening up. If it is too short it will interrupt you without reducing your fatigue or replenishing your energy.

Now you can see why an hour or two before breakfast is the 'best time' for many people. You get the benefit of the natural surge of energy at dawn. There is also a break prospect in the shape of the aptly named breakfast, the best and most energizing meal of the day for many of us. Above all, the rest of the world seems to still be asleep and so you have solitude and silence. There are still more benefits. Once your mental engine is running and warm, it is easy to keep going fast and hard after breakfast during that key period between 9am and noon. Finally, it is difficult not to feel a sense of self-satisfaction that you have managed to get up early and have been productive while others have slept away the best of the day.

A possible disadvantage if you make getting up early a habit is that you will feel even more tired than usual at 3pm and positively sleepy at dinner. You may be able to take a nap at lunch. Or you may find as you grow older that you can manage on less sleep anyway. If not, there is no rule that says you must always get up each day at the same time. Flexibility of mind and a good alarm clock is all you need.

HOW TO BE MORE CREATIVE

Creative thinking cannot be forced. If you are working on a problem and getting nowhere, it is often best to leave it for a while and let your subconscious mind take over. Your mind does not work by the clock although it likes deadlines. Sometimes the answer will come to you in the middle of the night.

Grasping the principle of the 'depth mind' – as I call the subconscious and unconscious part of the brain – could open the door for you to make the best use of your best time. Many people are still not even aware that their depth minds can carry out important mental functions for them, such as synthesizing parts into new wholes or establishing new connections while they are engaged in other activities.

Imagine your mind is like an email inbox. It would be great if you could sit down for an hour each morning before breakfast and receive inspired emails from your depth mind. But it isn't like that. The inbox might start receiving messages at any time of the day or night.

The whole creative thinking process can be described thus:

PREPARATION   The hard work. You have to collect and sort the relevant information, analyse the problem as thoroughly as you can, and explore possible solutions.

INCUBATION   This is the depth mind phase. Mental work – analysing, synthesizing and valuing – continues on the problem in our subconscious mind. The parts of the problem separate and new combinations occur. These may involve other ingredients stored away in your memory.

INSIGHT   The 'Eureka' moment. A new idea emerges into your conscious mind, either gradually or suddenly like a fish flashing out of the water. These moments often occur when you are not thinking about the problem but are in a relaxed frame of mind.

VALIDATION   This is where your valuing faculty comes into play. A new idea, insight, intuition,

hunch or solution needs to be thoroughly
tested. This is especially so if it is to form
the basis for action of any kind.

If you are using prime time for thinking along a certain line
and nothing happens, stop. Instead of investing more time –
throwing good money after bad – analyse the problem again
and see if you can come up with a new approach. Usually
your frustration will be caused by one of the mental road-
blocks in the table opposite.

The processes of analysing a problem or identifying an
objective are themselves means of programming the mind.
Possible solutions and courses of action almost instantly
begin to occur to us. Where there is a time delay this means
that the deeper parts of the brain have been summoned into
action and have made what contribution they can.

So you believe in the depth mind? By belief I don't mean
that you are merely prepared to assent to the proposition
that it exists, or even that it can work creatively for some
people. By belief I mean something akin to personal faith.
Do you *trust* your depth mind? Do you accept that it can,
does and will work for you?

If your answer is an unreserved 'Yes' or a more cautious
'I hope so' or 'I would like to think so', some consequences
for action follow. The fundamental principle is to work with
nature, not against it. In *Effective Decision Making* I describe
the natural processes of the mind at work, including the
depth mind dimension. In this companion book you can see
how important *preparation time* is for creative thinking:
careful and clear analysis, conscious imagining or synthesizing – using such techniques as brainstorming and solo
brainstorming – and exercising the valuing function of
thought in a positive rather than negative way.

If you are planning to experiment and try a session before

MENTAL ROADBLOCKS	
Lack of facts	If you are not sure you have all the relevant and available facts, you naturally hesitate to commit yourself. Do some more research and that may get you moving again.
Lack of conviction	Maybe you are finding it difficult because you lack conviction in this particular project or the way in which you have been asked to do it. Re-establish a worthwhile objective.
Lack of a starting point	Possibly the task seems so large that you don't know where to start. If so, make a start anywhere. You can always change it later. Inspiration comes after you've started, not before.
Lack of perspective	Perhaps you are too close to the problem, especially if you have lived with it for a long time or have been worrying about it incessantly. Try leaving it for a week. Consult others. Simply explaining it to them may help. They may see new angles.
Lack of motivation	Do you want it to happen enough? Creative thinking requires perseverance in the face of surmountable difficulty. If you are too easily put off it may be a sign that deep down you lack the necessary motivation. Reinvigorate your sense of purpose.

breakfast it is useful always to have a preparation phase the night before. Imagine yourself as a decorator, scraping down the woodwork, filling in holes and priming prior to painting the first coat on the following day.

MOONLIGHTING

Sometimes you will find that you awaken naturally in the early hours of the morning and then lie awake with ideas tumbling over each other in your mind. Again, be flexible. Resist the idea that you must go back to sleep simply because you are in bed and beds are for sleeping. Instead, make notes about the ideas while they are fresh in your mind – you will need to keep a notepad by your bed for this purpose. Then you can go back to sleep. Moonlighting – in the context of this book – has also been found, paradoxically, to be an excellent cure for insomnia.

THE PARETO PRINCIPLE

The Pareto principle, named after an Italian economist, states that the significant items of a given group form a relatively small part of the total. For example, 20 per cent of the sales force will bring in 80 per cent of new business. As that ratio seems to hold true in many areas, it is often called the 80:20 rule or the concept of 'the vital few and trivial many'.

Other writers have already applied this principle to time management. It is especially useful in coping with daily lists of action points. Most of the benefits will be related to two or three of the items. Select these key items and allocate blocks of consolidated time to achieve them.

The Pareto principle also relates to the time available in your day: 80 per cent of your really productive and creative work will be done in 20 per cent of your time. Not just any old 20 per cent. By now you should know clearly which four or five hours of the day constitute your prime time.

KEY POINTS: MAKING BEST USE OF YOUR BEST TIME

- Your best time is simply when you do your best work. For most people it is early in the morning, with performance tailing off by lunchtime. Use this time for your most important work. The early bird usually catches the worm.

- You will get the most out of your prime hours if you give some study to the laws of creative thinking. Preparation in the form of problem analysis and information collecting is especially valuable. Understanding how your mind works, especially the depth mind principle, is a great help. It enables you to work with nature and not against it.

- 'Chance only favours invention for minds that are prepared for it by patient study and persevering efforts,' wrote French microbiologist Louis Pasteur.

- Most of us have experienced solutions to problems that have come when we have 'slept on it'. In other words, silently but surely your depth mind has been working for you. Creative ideas often come when you are working early in the morning. Be ready to catch them like a fisherman waiting on a riverbank.

- Moonlighting, in this book, means working in bed in the small hours of the morning. If your mental activity looks like being fruitful, turn the light on and take some notes. One entrepreneur dreamt of a brilliant new product but forgot to write the dream down. Next day he had forgotten it and was furious with himself. Fortunately he had the same dream the next night and wrote it down. Now he is a millionaire.

- About 20 per cent of your time will produce 80 per cent of your productive output. Can you afford not to manage

at least *that* 20 per cent? Start tomorrow with those four
or five hours and it will change your life.

Mind, it is our best work that He wants, not the dregs of
our exhaustion. I think He must prefer quality to quantity.
                                    George MacDonald, Scottish author

8

TIME EFFECTIVENESS IN OFFICES

Many of us work in offices. These range from palatial suites in the headquarters of large organizations to the single room of a professional or self-employed person.

As you progress in managing your time well you will increasingly become aware of the dangers posed by office life. For offices are inhabited by other people. They may not use their own time to good effect. Even worse, they may misuse your time or frustrate your efforts in a hundred ways.

Don't misunderstand me; I believe passionately in the value of working with others. Teamwork is an essential and enjoyable element in most jobs. But there is a vast difference between the rare phenomenon of a high performance team and most work groups. One key characteristic of such a team is that each individual team member uses both his or her own time and the time of the other members to good effect.

Just as many products now carry a public health warning, so certain offices should also carry a time warning: 'WORK-ING IN THIS OFFICE COULD DAMAGE YOUR TIME'.

Whether or not your office comes into this category does not simply depend upon the attitudes and skills of your colleagues or staff. Imagine for a moment that your office is a watering hole in the African bush. Predators know where to find game at these places at certain hours. Major time-wasters equally know where you will be if they are hungry for your lifeblood of time.

The object of this chapter is to help you to transform your office into a platform for effective action. After reading it you should be clear about the principles of time management in offices and have some ideas about applying them next week to your own office.

OFFICE ARRANGEMENT

Time can be wasted imperceptibly if your work area isn't organized well. Of course you shouldn't become obsessed with office furnishings. A symptom of a status-conscious person is precisely this constant anxiety over the quality of the carpet or size of a desk. But you should strive to develop a well-ordered office, one that will allow you maximum freedom to pursue your work effectively.

As an individual you will naturally differ from others in your likes and dislikes over office organization. Work habits vary. But you should test your habits against the consensus of the habits of successful executives given below. It may be that you have picked up some bad ones on the way. If so, these malfunctioning routines need modifying, if not dropping altogether.

Your office should be arranged in the light of the functions you perform. Equipment and materials that you use most often need to be close to you. If you need to print or photocopy things frequently each day, for example, the relevant machines should be within easy reach – not where you have to disturb other things or people to get to them.

Physical comfort and aesthetic satisfaction are important

factors. You may have walked into your office sometimes and been depressed by the disorder: papers piled high, yesterday's coffee cups, dust and dirt, unwashed windows and dreary decoration. Change it. It is surprising how much better everyone feels if the office is freshly decorated, the walls lightened and hung with some cheerful or motivating pictures or prints.

Good lighting is especially important in order to prevent tired eyes and headaches. Desk-level lighting should always be considered, for it is more concentrated than overhead lighting. It also cuts down on noise, as people tend to walk slower and talk lower in areas of localized light.

Never grudge the expense of buying comfortable and well-designed chairs for yourself and your staff. Backache and now repetitive strain are common ailments and can seriously afflict those who sit for long hours in badly designed chairs, especially if working on a computer for hours at a time. Take expert advice and buy chairs and other office furniture that enable people to work without straining their backs or inducing unnecessary physical fatigue.

The actual plan of your office should be reviewed. If you are a more senior manager or executive, your office should ideally be arranged with a working area and a meeting area. A possible office design is shown overleaf.

Your desk should be placed so that you have to turn away from it in order to face and talk to a visitor. If you talk to a person over a desk it can seem a barrier – if not a barricade – between the two of you.

If you do much writing and are right-handed, the source of daylight should normally come from the left. Not having the window directly in front of you may also cut down on possible distractions from outside.

An adequate work surface is essential. In this respect an office is like a kitchen. A desk is insufficient. You will also

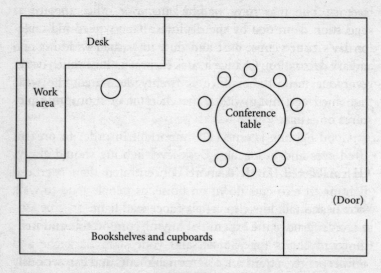

Office Design

need a work table or counter adjoining your desk or immediately behind you.

If you travel extensively, somewhere to hang clothes and keep luggage can save time. If you lack a suitable annexe to your office for this purpose a small wardrobe can provide enough space.

You may notice that the conference table in the diagram above is a round one. Remember the legendary King Arthur and his famous round table. Unlike an oblong table, Arthur's round one helped prevent tiresome quarrels about pecking order among his knights. Nobody could argue that they were placed below the salt, or that someone else was nearer the king.

A round table symbolizes a high degree of equality. It emphasizes the true nature of council, which is that all should speak their minds without fear or favour. 'When we have a problem,' wrote one Shell manager, who accepted a suggestion from one of his employees to buy a round table for his office, 'we get together the best people to address it and we are all equals in that discussion. Often we get very good ideas from the more junior people and it is important that they feel free to participate. Somehow a round table seems both practical and appropriate.'

THE ART OF DESKMANSHIP

Your desk should be clear of all paper except the specific job in hand. That invites you to think about one thing at a time. Concentration is a great time-saver.

Take an objective look at your desk the next time you sit down at it. Is there a clutter of papers, letters and files sitting on it? If left, unmolested clutter creates in you a feeling of being 'snowed under', resulting in tension and frustration. As a first step, clear up your desk and files in order to cut down the amount of time needed to search for items. If in doubt ask yourself: 'What's the worst thing that will happen if I throw this away?'

Once your desk is clear check that it's organized so that you don't spend time searching for things like pens, paper-clips, ruler, scissors, stapler, paper, envelopes, memo pads, phone chargers and so on. Remember again the wise old rule: *A place for everything and everything in its place.*

Think of your desk as both a workbench and tool chest. Many managers act as if their desks are four-sided waste-paper baskets, or storage depots for odds and ends, or flat surfaces for stacking correspondence and files. One manager, who kept a careful record of his time, discovered one week that he had spent one hour and seventeen minutes searching for key papers on top of or in the drawers of his desk!

PAPERWORK

Having sorted through your files and weeded out the papers that can be safely thrown away, you are now ready to tackle new papers – the material that arrives in various forms on your desk each day.

The principle that is often recommended is *to handle each piece of paper only once*. It's been called the million pound idea. Managers who have discovered and applied it have saved up to one hour a day or 220 hours a year. Don't put down a letter or memo or close an email that needs a response until you have fired off a reply. It's often easier to think of an answer when you've just read a letter and your reaction is fresh in your mind.

Alternatively it has been suggested that anything worth reading deserves reading more than once. Certainly a decision will sometimes require more thought and you may not be able to reply at once. If so, do something to move ahead the project that the paper or electronic message alludes to, even if it's only a decision to seek advice or to determine when you'll review the matter again.

'Disposing' of a letter, report or email in this decisive way requires constant practice and an iron will. But it is the key to handling paperwork and so it is worth acquiring the habit.

If paper arrives by the sackload or your inbox is full to the brim after the weekend or a holiday, do not panic. Sort the daily mountain into piles according to priority, following the categories listed in the table opposite.

Put the highest priority from the immediate action pile in the centre of your desk and put the remainder on a work surface. You can only think about one thing at a time. You can only focus on one task at a time. Concentrate all your attention on that item.

THE PAPERWORK MOUNTAIN	
FOR ACTION	If you can take complete action, do so at once. If that is not possible, take action. Mark on it what action is needed, then consign to pending tray or file. This works electronically as well as with paper. Have an effective 'brought forward' system.
FOR INFORMATION	Read and then file, throw away or pass on duly initialled. Comment directly on the paper or track onto the electronic file wherever possible.
FOR READING	This is material that does not need to be read at once. Save it for marginal time. Use the folder facility on your computer to help you file things for later.
FOR WASTE PAPER	If the paper fits into none of the above categories consign it speedily to the wastepaper basket or computer trash facility – make sure this is emptied regularly to keep things tidy and save valuable memory space.

It is worth keeping a bottom drawer or file for paper that you deliberately want to leave alone unless someone asks for it. I call it the Procrastination Drawer.

Procrastination is a time-consuming habit, but calculated or deliberate procrastination is a weapon in your armoury. Use it selectively and occasionally. Some problems if left alone will solve themselves. If someone shouts for it, you can always say you have been studying it and then get down to work rapidly. It's a bit risky, but you can save hours tackling some tasks that may evaporate before you've done your required work. Review the drawer from time to time, and never use it to put off a task you know you should do.

A final rule: clearing your desk completely, or at least leaving it in good order, should become a habit. No good workman will ever leave his workbench strewn with blunt tools, wood shavings and pots of congealed glue at the end of the day. A clear desk is a foundation for tomorrow's work.

Paperwork: The Marks & Spencer method

In 1956 Sir Simon Marks, the chairman of Marks & Spencer, noticed two managers at one store working overtime checking stockcards. Marks found that a million of these cards were being filled in every year. After investigation it was found that these cards were not necessary and could be replaced by much simpler methods of inventory checking, such as spot checks. This set stockroom staff free to replenish supplies when stocks ran low.

This success led the company to launch a campaign against excessive paperwork. Every file, memo and form, every kind of paperwork was examined. Managers were asked: 'Would the business collapse if we dispensed with this form?'

Some 26 million pieces of paper or card, a total of 120 tons of paper, were eliminated in the first year. For example, time sheets were thrown away and the responsibility of ensuring good timekeeping was given to supervisors.

The principles of eliminating or simplifying paperwork have continued to be rigorously applied at Marks & Spencer. The guiding policy is: 'If in doubt, throw it out.'

The realization that people can be trusted to follow general guidelines is a cornerstone of the war against paperwork and paper. Otherwise, manuals of detailed instructions and written reports as the only means of control will multiply.

Another key principle is the idea of 'sensible approxima-tion'. It means that getting figures close enough for all practi-cal purposes makes more sense than seeking perfection. As Sir

Simon Marks said, 'Those who make a fetish out of perfection are wasting time and money which could be better allocated elsewhere.'

HOW TO WRITE AND READ EFFECTIVELY

While on the subject of paperwork it is worth reviewing your basic skills of writing and reading. Advanced proficiency in them is a sure way to conserve your time.

Let's start with writing skills, for you are a generator of paperwork through your pen or keyboard and printer as well as a consumer of it. In the ongoing war on paper and paperwork, are you part of the solution or are you part of the problem?

Clarity, simplicity and conciseness are the essentials of business writing. If you can add to them strength, vigour and tone you will produce high-quality papers or letters. You will also be able to write more of them in less time.

How do you develop the habit of clear, simple and concise writing? One method is to discipline yourself to follow a systematic approach, whether you are dictating a letter or writing a paper. Aim first for an orderly outline, as shown in the table overleaf.

Do not cover too many subjects in one letter, as you run the risk of overloading the reader with information. Remember that the reader will tend to fasten attention on the most interesting point and disregard your other 'pearls of wisdom'.

Keep it short and simple. Shortness is achieved by not overburdening the reader with too much data. Edit out any irrelevant, overlong or repetitive sentences. Strive to write one-page letters or memos – they are more digestible. For your reader's sake avoid jargon, ambiguity and formal

STEPS TO CLARITY OF EXPRESSION	
THINK	What is my purpose in writing? Pinpoint the message. Find the heart of the letter you are answering. Underline the key issue or question that should be answered. Try to visualize the reader.
LIST	Jot down each thought that you want to express on a scrap of paper.
ARRANGE	Put your points in a logical order, discarding the irrelevant ones.

language. Write conversationally, using short sentences and familiar words.

Reading skills once acquired can save time. Speed-reading courses are not the answer. It is better to save time by cutting out all reading that is only of marginal value than to learn to gallop through everything by speed-reading methods.

Now that the photocopier and computerized printer have added immeasurably to the paper that is produced and distributed in organizations, it is essential to develop your ability to scan through, say, a report quickly and accurately. Do not assume that you must read every word. Treat it like a newspaper. Start with the headlines on the cover. Then look at the introduction, where the author tells you his or her aims and the method he or she has adopted. Then glance at the table of contents. Try to identify the key ideas in each chapter or section. Read details only when they are related to a key idea important to you. Using this method, you can become proficient at gutting a report or book in a remarkably short time. If you use a computer, you could always use scroll, zoom and page-finder tools to scan a report quickly, without having to print it out.

Don't always read at top gear. Occasionally you may come

across a passage, paper or book that will be profoundly useful to you in the future. Don't rush through it now. Read it once or twice at your leisure, making notes on it. By this method its message will become a part of you.

MAKE THE TELEPHONE WORK FOR YOU

The telephone is a great time-saving tool – in the right hands. By using it you can obtain information that would take you days or weeks by letter. Not only can it save time but a telephone conversation can also cut down the considerable expenses of travel. Unlike a letter it gives you the opportunity for spoken dialogue with the other person. It is usually inferior in value to an actual meeting but it is often better than correspondence. And with the invention of the conference call, group meetings – between a team, council or committee or with clients – are even possible over the phone, with the addition of live video links in some cases! This can save further time by eliminating the need to call each person separately.

How much time do you spend on the telephone? Some research suggests that managers can overestimate or underestimate the time taken up in this way by as much as 50 per cent. This is especially true today with the advent of mobile telephones, SMS texting and instant messaging services. If you haven't done so already try keeping a time log specifically of your telephone time – both incoming and outgoing calls – for one week. Use a stopwatch to give some precision to your self-study. You can also use itemized telephone bills to confirm or emphasize how long you spend on the phone each day, week or month.

Your first reaction to these results may be: 'I didn't know I talked that long.' Here are some rules of thumb for making better use of the telephone:

Planning   Make a habit of planning each telephone call that you make, using an abbreviated form of the system suggested above for letters. Make a brief note of what you want to say or what you wish to find out, so that the object of the call is clear in your mind. This will save both your time and the time of the person on the other end of the telephone. Your aim is concise, clear and friendly communication.

Batching   Set aside a period of time each day for making and – if possible – receiving telephone calls. By bunching your calls before lunch or towards the end of the day, when people are less inclined towards verbosity, you can get through your telephoning much more economically.

Timing   Buy an egg timer – the sandglass variety – and place it by the telephone. Aim to complete every telephone conversation in three minutes without introducing a sense of haste or, worse still, a tone of brusqueness. Keep a score and see if you can reduce your failure rate each week.

But don't forget there is a flip side. Telephone control makes practical good sense, especially if you are someone who has become addicted to your mobile phone or texting. A productivity rise of no less than 23 per cent in one year was reported by the Northwestern Mutual Life Insurance Company after the introduction of a quiet hour one day a week, when incoming telephone calls were shut off to let work continue uninterrupted. You could implement your own quiet hour or even half-day by activating the 'do not disturb' or 'divert calls' facility on your landline or mobile phone.

The same applies to emails and the Internet. Working

online can save huge amounts of time for many people but it's easy to get into bad habits: endless pressing of the 'send and receive' button, writing personal messages or surfing the web for information you don't need. Social or networking sites, while extremely useful to some businesses, should also be approached with an equal level of caution – some companies have had to ban the use of networking sites in the office when it was revealed that personal usage of sites was cutting into paid work time. Keeping an eye on your telephone or email usage is all part of managing your time – remember the old adage: 'A place for everything and everything in its place.'

HOW TO CONTROL INTERRUPTIONS

'Time is a dressmaker specializing in alterations,' said the writer Faith Baldwin. Much of your time will be taken up with unplanned alterations. Your carefully planned day can often end in shreds.

To repeat a point made earlier, don't assume that all interventions are interruptions of your time. You must look at so-called interruptions with perspective. What appears to be an interruption may well be a matter of high priority to the person interrupting. When you have listened, it may prove to be so for you too. In other words, there are good interruptions and bad ones. An act of judgement precedes your response. It filters interruptions, determining how much time, if any, you can give to each.

You can't eliminate interruptions. Many of them, as we have seen, are requests that you do whatever job you are being paid to do. Remember the on-call doctor mentioned earlier. It would be inappropriate for him or her to refuse to be interrupted when on call. Talking to patients, answering an anxious mother's question, responding to an emergency call – these are what the doctor's job is all about.

Still, you should plan in order to minimize the number of unwelcome interruptions if you're going to manage effectively. One hour of concentrated work is worth four hours broken into five-minute fragments by unwanted callers or trivial telephone queries; to re-immerse yourself in a report after each interruption takes time. So the real time cost of an interruption is much more than the actual time your visitor spends in your office.

Learning to manage these negative interruptions takes resolve and practice. Here are some guidelines for keeping interruptions as short as possible:

- Set a time limit and stick to it. Say: 'I have five minutes – will that do or would you rather fix a time for later?'
- Set the stage in advance; you are very busy with a deadline in sight.
- With casual droppers-in, remain standing. If they sit down, perch on the edge of your desk.
- Meet in the other person's office – you can then determine when to leave.
- Avoid small talk when you are busy; it doubles interruption time.
- Get them to the point. Don't be afraid to interrupt the interrupter, asking them what is the problem? What is the purpose of his or her call?
- Be ruthless with time but gracious with people. Give them your full attention. Listen well. Be firm but friendly and helpful. Do not let them go away empty-handed if you can avoid it.
- Have a clock available where visitors can see it, and don't be afraid to glance at it a few times. Explain about your next appointment; a white lie is better than a black interruption.

- Use a call-back system for telephone calls, unless they are important enough to be put through at once.

The person who interrupts you most in your office is – no, not your boss, he or she comes second – actually yourself. Sometimes we are all itching to be interrupted. Usually when you are tackling a chore or about to undertake an unpleasant task it is a delight to be interrupted. You wait for the telephone to ring. You check your emails hoping for a reason to stall the task in hand. Or you suddenly take it into your head to call up a colleague about a totally unimportant matter, thereby interrupting someone else: 'No, No, nothing urgent – just ringing for a chat.'

You can also interrupt yourself in a variety of extra-curricular ways: making coffee, dropping one project and starting another, surfing the Internet or networking sites, sending 'urgent' personal emails or text messages, gossiping with your secretary or a colleague, or keeping people too long at meetings. Despite protestations to the contrary you are 'asking for it'. You *need* interruptions. Beware of yourself, interruption master in disguise.

YOUR PROFESSIONAL ASSISTANT

Office secretary, personal assistant or PA: many are the names given to your professional assistant. By whatever name they are known they are vital to your success. His or her title should reflect the specific contribution that this person makes to the organization.

If your secretary has become part of your effective working team, then you have indeed a professional assistant, one who is a real asset both to you and the organization. He or she should be highly trained in all aspects of office management – communications and human relations as well as typing, filing and fielding calls. Today secretaries and PAs also need to be extremely well versed in relevant computer programmes and software packages. All these skills make them real professionals and chief time-savers in the office.

Most secretaries and PAs of today's chief executives already have a personal computer, personal digital assistant (PDA), one or two printers and possibly even closed-circuit TV – and the list grows as technology advances. Such secretaries spend less time serving coffee or typing and more time on administration, information collection and retrieval, and data interpretation, analysis, collection and presentation.

Simultaneously and somewhat ironically, personal computers and electronic mail can make it easier for a manager to type and send his own messages. Instead of reviewing their secretaries' work, some managers now find that their secretaries are checking their efforts at computing in its various forms. As technology advances at breakneck speed, it's not uncommon, for example, for the most junior secretaries or PAs to have a greater grasp of new computer programmes and how to use them than their senior counterparts or managers. A wise manager capitalizes on these skills and learns from them.

Office automation – using new technology to quickly perform certain tasks yourself, such as writing a report directly onto your computer rather than getting someone to type it out from handwritten notes – can free your secretary to perform essential administrative functions. These include helping you to save time by:

- Keeping unwanted callers at bay, on the telephone or in person. They may think they must see you, but if your PA is fully briefed he or she may be able to divert them to the appropriate person.

- Minimizing interruptions. Your PA can arrange interviews at times you have reserved for that purpose in your diary or arrange for you to telephone people at times convenient to you.
- Dealing with routine correspondence him or herself. Forms can be filled in or applications for such things as parking permits can be dealt with instead of landing on your desk.

Your professional assistant can only help you to manage your time better if you respect his or her time. That means refraining from needless interrupting. Try to bunch your requests, so that your PA has time to get on with jobs. Avoid chopping and changing your mind about priorities once you've told him or her what to do.

Use a pocket dictaphone or similar device to deal with non-automated correspondence, unless you need your secretary's input to the letter in question. You can dictate letters by the batch when it suits you, on a train journey for example, and your secretary can type them when it suits him or her.

Don't be a perfectionist. The less you fuss over details the better. Excellence is not the same as perfection. A good office team will strive for excellence but eschew the expensive and illusory goal of perfection. Nothing frustrates a secretary or PA more than a perfectionist manager, who must dot every 'i' and cross every 't' him or herself.

In short, your secretary or PA is an integral part of a work team. Treat them as a professional, not as a servant. Delegate to them as you would to other members of your team and respect their areas of responsibility while retaining overall accountability.

KEY POINTS: TIME EFFECTIVENESS IN OFFICES

- Take a close look at your office when you next go into it. Have you organized it, or does it organize you?
- A desk is a workbench for paperwork. Check that it is cleared for action at the end of each day. The essential tools of your trade should be readily at hand, so that you don't waste time searching for things.
- Work out a system for sorting incoming paper and electronic files or documents. See if you can apply the principle of handling each piece of paper only once.
- Just like driving a car, writing and reading can be done with skill. Clear, simple and concise writing saves your time and the time of your readers. With practice you can also learn to read faster: by swiftly and accurately recognizing what not to read or what can be scanned rather than absorbed.
- Telephones and electronic communication devices such as emails or texts are potentially great time-savers. In the wrong hands they can fragment your day.
- Distinguish between interruptions. Some are good; some are tolerable; and some are avoidable. A conscious act of judgement should govern your response. Once you are interrupted, employ some of the damage-control hints given in this chapter.
- The mirror will always reveal to you the number one interrupter in your life – you.
- If you have a secretary or PA, transform him or her into a professional assistant. Such a person has a strategic importance in the battle to use your time wisely within office hours.

> *Time wastes our bodies and our wits,*
> *But we waste Time, so we are quits.*
> Writing on a sundial from 1746

9

MANAGING MEETINGS

'Meetings, always meetings' sums up what you may think about meetings. Do the meetings you attend seem like a necessary evil, distracting you from your main business?

Attending too many badly organized meetings certainly engenders that attitude. If the basis for getting together is dubious in the first place, if the discussion drags on and the conclusions are unclear, it is not surprising that the overall experience is negative. 'What a waste of valuable time,' you mutter to yourself as the doors finally open.

What is a meeting? Here the word means a pre-planned arrangement for people to come together at a given time and place to do something, such as exchange information or make a decision. Meetings are distinguished here from interviews, which are basically on a one-to-one basis. The key principles of meetings, set out below, do apply to interviews as well. But other factors – such as question-asking technique – also have to be taken into account. Although unplanned or informal meetings and interviews do take up a great deal of your time, this chapter will only focus upon programmed meetings of more than two people.

There are, of course, many positive aspects to meetings. You cannot run any work group, team or organization without them. They are necessary, even essential, and often enjoyable – for we are social beings who delight in conversational give and take with each other. But meetings are still potential time-wasters. Other people may be more in control of the meeting than you are, and they may be cavalier with your time. Even if you are in the chair you may find that there is pressure upon you to extend the meeting unduly or even to hijack it for purposes other than the stated objectives.

The remedy for these potential time hazards lies in developing our skills both as leader – chairman – and as a team member. Do your meetings always, as a matter of policy, begin on time and end on time? Acquire the ability to budget accurately the time requirement in advance. Remember Parkinson's Law. Always negotiate time limits with other participants when they arrive before getting down to business: it will focus everyone's minds and energies to work to an agreed deadline.

DIFFERENT KINDS OF MEETINGS

In order to practise and perfect these time management skills it is useful to recognize the main categories of meetings in working life, as listed in the table opposite. Each has its particular nature and challenges. In real life any given meeting may have elements of two or three of the following types, but you will save time and conserve effort if you are able to make clear when you are changing gear from one to the other.

Council or collegiate meetings are worth a special mention because they are becoming more important as the professional knowledge and skill available in companies increases. Decisions in such meetings are usually made by consensus. That does not mean that the decision in question is a given member's preferred solution. But it does mean he or she will

FIVE TYPES OF MEETINGS

A BRIEFING MEETING
A briefing meeting is called by the manager to direct or instruct his or her team members to undertake a particular task or to lay down policy governing future conduct. It is characterized by:
- Giving instructions and information
- Clearing up misunderstandings
- Integrating ideas and views where appropriate

AN ADVISORY MEETING
An advisory meeting is called essentially for the exchange of information. It is not a decision making meeting as such. It is characterized by:
- Seeking advice about a problem
- Informing others about ideas
- Listening to views

A COUNCIL MEETING
A council meeting is held between people of equal standing who have some professional knowledge or skill to contribute to the matter in hand. It is characterized by:
- Decisions being made by consensus
- Accountability lying with the group
- Resolving differences by 'talking through' them

A COMMITTEE MEETING
A committee meeting is one in which representatives from various groups or interests meet on a roughly equal footing to make decisions on matters of common concern. It is characterized by:
- A sense of authority
- Differences ultimately being resolved by voting
- Compromises being common

A NEGOTIATING MEETING
A negotiating meeting is also one in which representatives of different interests meet, but decisions are made more on a bargaining basis than by voting. It is characterized by:
- Decisions being taken on a *quid pro quo* basis
- Each side having different but overlapping aims
- Each side seeking to achieve best terms for itself

accept it as the optimum decision in the situation and *be prepared to act upon it*. If members fail to implement a decision without cause it is a sure sign that the meeting reached a false consensus.

If a person disagrees at any point, he or she has to make clear their reason and contribute towards an alternative course of action that would be generally acceptable. For example, in a meeting on the construction of a new building there needs to be a consensus between the accountants, architects and builders. If the accountants told the architects that the proposed building was too expensive in terms of the company's funds, then a joint reappraisal would have to be done. It would be senseless for the architects and builders to ignore the accountants. It would be equally inappropriate for the accountants to turn a deaf ear to what the builders had to say about safety standards. They have to work it through until a consensus is reached on what is the optimum building, one that will yield an acceptable profit, meet the needs of the customer, look good and be completely safe.

The distinctive feature of the work of a council-type of meeting is that several minds in cooperation, on the basis of a substantial degree of equality, are needed to make the decision. The decision is therefore the decision of the group as a whole and each member is bound by it. He or she may have to accept a decision even though in disagreement. If the matter does not permit a compromise, it is his or her duty to resign in this instance. For this reason, in a well-conducted council meeting it should seldom be found necessary to take a vote. If the chairman cannot sum up the sense of the meeting in a form that participating members will accept, the matter is probably not yet ripe for decision by that body. This is, in fact, what happens at meetings of most boards of directors; only very occasionally is a vote taken.

The way people sit at tables and the shape of the table itself can tell much about the purpose of the meeting. The round table aptly symbolizes and best serves the council type of meeting. It emphasizes the lack of a pecking order: all seats around it but one – that of the leader – are of equal importance. In Chapter Eight, I suggested that the round table should become more of a feature in managers' offices. Many innovative individual managers and companies have already disposed of their square tables – symbols of hierarchical models of management – and introduced round tables into their offices. For a round table encourages a team approach to decision making and problem solving, with the leader leading by competence – not because he or she sits at the head of the table.

It is important that meetings should be used for the purpose for which they are best suited. Two matters on which a committee decision may well be more valuable than an individual's decision are:

1 Questions of general policy or major decisions where the interplay of various interests and factors needs to be balanced; these tend to be matters that do not require immediate decisions and when a period of gestation may be valuable. However, there are plenty of examples of committees that take decisions more quickly than could be done by individual consultation.

2 Matters that for various reasons need to be de-personalized; for example, where personal predilection and bias need to run the gauntlet of criticism by others and to be recognized as having done so.

THE COST OF MEETING

Managers spend much time in meetings of all kinds and consequently meetings are expensive. It is important to develop a sense of the financial cost of meetings as a step towards the better management both of your time and of the time of other people. The following chart gives you a picture of the cost of a person's time in ratio to their salary:

THE COST OF YOUR TIME				
The following figures are based on a working year of 238 days with one working day equal to seven hours. Overheads are not included. The chart highlights how costly time-wasting can be at various salary levels.				
Salary/Annum £	5 mins	15 mins	1 hour	1 day
35,000	£1.75	£5.25	£21.00	£147.00
30,000	£1.50	£4.50	£18.00	£126.00
25,000	£1.25	£3.75	£15.00	£105.00
20,000	£1.00	£3.00	£12.00	£84.00
15,000	£0.75	£2.25	£9.00	£63.00

The obvious question to ask yourself before every meeting is:

IS THIS MEETING REALLY NECESSARY?

All too often people meet for the sake of meeting. Getting together at regular times becomes a habit. It is possible that the original purpose for that particular group of people to come together has been fulfilled. Or the purpose may need redefinition – if so, you should review who should be involved as well as the place and time of the meeting.

Before you call your next meeting consider the other options, not least because they are more economical in money as well as time: could the matter be dealt with by letter, memo, telephone calls, emails or meetings with individuals? Sometimes ten minutes spent with six people individually is more productive than trying to get them all together for an hour.

Check on the composition of the meeting. Make sure the meeting isn't larger than it needs to be. Do all managers need to attend all meetings? Be wary of arguments like 'They always come along' or 'We can't risk offence by not inviting him' or 'You never can tell, we might just need her'. The presence of too many people cuts down the time each individual has to contribute to the discussion.

It is a good idea to review all the meetings you attend – especially those you attend on a regular basis – at least twice a year.

The 'Regular meeting analysis sheet' overleaf is designed to help you to do this review. As a result of completing the sheet with a particular committee meeting in mind you may decide, for example, that you can safely switch from regular to occasional attendance; or from being there for the whole meeting to attending only for those items on the agenda that concern you or your department. Information about the other business can usually be gleaned from the minutes – if they are properly kept and circulated – in a way that is much more time-efficient for you.

With meetings in mind may I remind you of the importance of learning to say no (see page 70). People often accumulate regular meeting commitments because they cannot bring themselves to say no in the first place or to extricate themselves from meetings they have unwisely agreed to attend. Over-commitment soon leads to ineffectiveness.

REGULAR MEETING ANALYSIS SHEET

MEETING:

PURPOSE (in one sentence):

MEMBERS:

FREQUENCY:

AVERAGE DURATION:

RANK IMPORTANCE (on a scale of 0 = Useless to 10 = Absolutely essential):

  (i)   To me:

  (ii) To organization:

COMMENTS:

SHOULD I ATTEND: Full time   Action required:

                       Part time

                       Occasionally

                       Not at all

DATE FOR NEXT REVIEW:

PREPARING FOR AN EFFECTIVE MEETING

Careful preparation is the secret of time-effective meetings. First and foremost, it is essential that the chairman be clear about the objective or objectives of the proposed meeting. It may be one of any of the 'Five types of meetings' identified on page 105, or a combination of them. Within those categories the actual purpose needs to be crystal clear. A useful way of double-checking is to ask yourself: 'Where should we all be at the end of this meeting?'

The agenda is a key factor. It shouldn't just be a list of headings to jog your memory during a meeting. Draw it up with thought, indicating whether an item is for discussion or decision. Briefly describe the matter or subject. 'Mounting costs', for example, looks too brief and vague, whereas 'Mounting costs: to discuss the report on energy conservation in the factory and make decisions on the first and third recommendations on p. 16 of this report' is much more definite. It gives people the opportunity to think about the matter beforehand. Ensure that everyone receives the agenda and relevant papers – in this case the energy conservation report – at least five clear days before the meeting.

People take in information more readily through their eyes than their ears. Hence the Chinese proverb, 'A picture is worth a thousand words'. Therefore visual aids should more often than not play a part in your meetings: if they are clear, simple and vivid they can save you time.

EXERCISE 2: Be prepared
Identify the next three formal meetings that you will chair. Jot them down on a piece of paper and label them A, B and C. Do you intend to make use of any of the following:

	A	B	C
Projector	—	—	—
Slideshow	—	—	—
Prepared flipcharts/whiteboard	—	—	—
Unprepared flipcharts/whiteboard	—	—	—
Audiovisual equipment (TV/DVD)	—	—	—
3D visual aids	—	—	—
Communications equipment	—	—	—
Reports	—	—	—
Financial statements	—	—	—
A written agenda	—	—	—

Models   ___ ___ ___
Minutes   ___ ___ ___
A different room layout   ___ ___ ___

The key preliminary steps can be summarized in the following way:

PREPARING FOR MEETINGS
DETERMINE PURPOSE OF MEETINGS Consider possible aims, such as: • To engage in joint consultation • To develop support for action • To resolve unsolved problems EXPLORE THE SUBJECT Collect/research facts and information Identify main topics to be discussed Consider probable differences in viewpoint OUTLINE THE DISCUSSION Set final objective Consider intermediate objectives Frame questions to develop discussion Plan introduction specially, include main topics for discussion Prepared timetable for meeting HAVE EVERYTHING READY Issue invitations and information in good time Arrange accommodation Prepare necessary materials, include aids such as flipcharts or digital presentations

Time spent on preparation is seldom wasted. If you go into a meeting clear about the objectives, having thought about the subject in advance and with everything ready, it is already most probable that your time will be well spent.

TIMETABLING THE MEETINGS

The agenda is so important as a time-conserving instrument that it merits special attention here. If you are the chairman it constitutes your plan for the meeting.

Minutes of the previous meeting should usually be circulated in advance and not read through at the meeting itself. Checking the minutes should not take long. If any substantial matters arise from them they should be noted and dealt with later in the meeting according to their level of urgency and importance.

Much time will also have been saved, as already noted, if you have circulated papers or data in advance. If this has not been possible, table it at the meeting. Having circulated a paper, however, don't read it though line by line – assume others have done their homework.

The order of items on the agenda is important, especially if the outcome of discussing one item will influence the decision on another.

Non-controversial subjects may be grouped at the beginning and the end of the meeting, so that it begins and ends on a high note. You must ensure that important subjects are discussed at a time when minds are fresh, usually towards the head of the agenda.

To reiterate the first and most important point in this chapter: always try to fix finishing times for meetings. If you are the chairman say at the outset, 'Do you think we can get this meeting over by such-and-such a time?' If you are not in the chair ask, 'Have you any idea what time this meeting will end?' Everyone will have the target finishing time in their minds and you will find that this concentrates their minds and prevents long-windedness. Otherwise the principle that work expands to fill the time available for it will insinuate itself into your meeting.

Within that overall time framework – which more often than not should be agreed before people assemble and should appear on the agenda – it is good practice to allocate a time to each item and make sure that this time is not grossly exceeded. Some flexibility is essential, and so you should always build into your time plan a contingency reserve of minutes that can be drawn upon at your discretion.

THE CHAIRMAN'S ROLE

Good chairmanship is vital for time-saving meetings. The chairman's task will sometimes pose problems, but a good chairman can make sure that a meeting is punctual, covers the agenda properly and achieves its objects. He or she uses other people's time economically and effectively.

As a chairman yourself it is useful to bear in mind that you have two principal functions within your role. Being chairman in the narrow sense means you are accountable for seeing that procedures are adhered to and that participants both behave themselves and contribute as effectively as possible to the business in hand. You are there to see fair play, to ensure that everyone has their turn, and to apply the appropriate rules, not unlike a referee. The foreman of a jury is a chairman in this specific sense.

Secondly, you may be the group's leader or manager as well, charged with achieving specified results. The nature of those outcomes will necessarily vary according to the type of meeting (see the 'Five types of meetings' table on page 105). In creative thinking meetings, for example, the leader's role may be more that of a catalyst than traffic controller.

There can be some obvious tensions between the 'referee' and 'leader' roles. Some groups and leaders indeed seek to avoid them by appointing a referee-type chairman, like the Speaker in the House of Commons, leaving leaders free to argue their case in the meeting without having to preside over it. Other chairmen signal when they are changing hats by stepping down from the chair for a particular item on the agenda.

In most situations it makes sense for the chairman to exercise both functions. There is some overlap between the two roles anyway. Let us assume here that you are doing both.

Some of the key leadership functions, such as *defining the task* and *planning*, have been previously discussed. But as chairman you should remember to begin the meeting by saying what the purpose is and why it is necessary. Don't assume that everyone knows. You may also want to check that the participants are comfortable with the agenda, so that *your* plan for the meeting now becomes *our* plan for it. In a pleasant but firm way, show that you have taken charge.

Once work has started on the agenda you will have to exercise the function of *controlling*, which should be done with intelligence and sensitivity. What would you do about an over-talkative person? It is essential to stop him or her but it has to be done tactfully as well as firmly: 'Thank you, Michael, I think we get the drift of your argument. Susan, you haven't said anything yet. Do you agree with Michael or not?' If a long-winded person still challenges you for the right of way – by continuing to talk over others or by interrupting again – then you will have to show more steel until the message is taken. Never lose control.

CONTROLLING THE CABINET

The Cabinet usually meets once a week. That should be enough for regular meetings, and should be if they grasp from the start what they are there for. They should be back at their work as soon as possible, and a Prime Minister should put as little as possible in their way. We started sharp at 11, and rose in time for lunch. Even in a crisis, another couple of meetings should be enough in the same week: if there is a crisis, the less talk the better.

The Prime Minister shouldn't speak too much himself in Cabinet. He should start the show or ask somebody else to do so, and then intervene only to bring out the more modest chaps who, despite their seniority, might say nothing if not asked. And the Prime Minister must sum up. Experienced Labour leaders should be pretty good at this; they have spent years attending debates at meetings of the Parliamentary Party and the National Executive, and have to sum *those* up. That takes some doing – good training for the Cabinet.

Particularly when a non-Cabinet Minister is asked to attend, especially if it is his first time, the Prime Minister may have to be cruel. The visitor may want to show how good he is, and go on too long. A good thing is to take no chance and ask him to send the Cabinet a paper in advance. The Prime Minister can then say, 'A very clear statement, Minister. Do you need to add anything?' in a firm tone of voice obviously expecting the answer, '*No*'. If somebody else looks like making a speech, it is sound to nip in with 'Has anybody any objection?' If somebody starts to ramble, a quick, '*Are you objecting?* You're not? Right. Next business,' and the Cabinet can move on.

Clement Attlee, UK prime minister (1945–51)

Heading off potential or actual irrelevancies is also a vital part of controlling a meeting. Sometimes a red herring looks tastier than the bread-and-butter items on the agenda. Where the object of a meeting is creative thinking, it is often worth pursuing apparent red herrings. For the apparently irrelevant may disguise a new idea, just as an oyster shell is the unlikely bed of a pearl.

To exercise these leadership functions and to contribute yourself to the discussion, you will need to develop yourself by becoming:

- A clear and rapid thinker
- An attentive listener
- Able to express yourself clearly and succinctly
- Ready to clarify views badly expressed
- Able to be impartial and impersonal
- A preventer of inappropriate interruptions
- Patient, tolerant and kind
- Friendly but brisk and businesslike

At the end of each item on the agenda the chairman should give a brief, clear and concise *summary* of what has been decided. He or she may even dictate the key sentence or phrase to be used in the minutes.

If someone is asked to take action as a result of discussion on an item, the chairman should check that the participant understands and accepts that action. Steps or actions thus agreed should normally carry a completion time.

The question sometimes asked as to whether a committee can be executive – meaning it can do anything on its own – is really trivial. As in the case of a football team scoring a goal there must be an individual agent, but it is the group that makes it possible for the individual to act. Although the group's decision will usually be carried out by one of its members, or its officers, in a real sense the action is the action of the committee. The important decision has been made by the committee, or is a consequence of its deliberations.

To ensure that action results from the work of a committee and to preserve personal responsibility, one method is to appoint a committee chairman who is not the most senior member there but one whose personal job responsibility is most in line with the responsibility of the committee.

THE ART OF MINUTING

As a guideline you as chairman should not take the minutes. That job should be delegated to your secretary, PA or other appropriate employee. If he or she cannot do the minutes this time then another group member should do them. If you attempt to do the minutes it will distract you from running the meeting smoothly.

Minutes do not have to be lengthy or complicated but they should cover the following key points:

- Time, date and place of meeting
- Names of those present and any apologies for absence
- All items discussed, together with conclusions reached, decisions made and actions agreed
- Names of those responsible for actions
- In some cases the main arguments or steps leading to decisions
- The time the meeting ended
- The date and time of the next meeting, and where it will be held

Minutes should be sent out within two or three days – or faster if technology allows – especially if there are some actions to be taken fairly soon after the meeting. If full minutes are needed yet cannot be produced that soon, then a summary of actions to be taken should be listed and distributed at once, either electronically or as a photocopy. As chairman you should ideally sign minutes before they are distributed.

MAKING MEETINGS EFFECTIVE	
	START ON TIME
AIM	OUTLINE PURPOSE CLEARLY State problem/situation/reason Define constraints and limitations Establish task(s) of meeting
GUIDE	ENSURE EFFECTIVE DISCUSSION Introduce topic(s) for discussion Draw out opinions, viewpoints and experiences Develop group interest and involvement Keep discussion within stated task(s)
CRYSTALLIZE	ESTABLISH CONCLUSIONS Recognize degrees of feeling and changes of opinion Summarize points of agreement and disagreement State intermediate conclusions as they are reached Check understanding and acceptance
ACT	GAIN ACCEPTANCE AND COMMITMENT Summarize and state conclusion(s) clearly Gain commitment to action plan State responsibility for action Make sure that everybody understands
	END ON TIME

A SELF-DEVELOPMENT EXERCISE

You should conclude this chapter with a review of your own performance at meetings. The following exercise should help you to pinpoint the areas for improvement. Transfer the headings below to a piece of blank paper or Word document, leaving space for your answers.

EXERCISE 3: A self-development exercise

In the role of chairman of meetings my strengths are:
(Only write down strengths that are corroborated by comments or feedback you have received from others, so that you are speaking from data.)

The five areas in which I must improve are:
(List here no more than five definite steps you can take to overcome your present weaknesses as a chairman.)

To improve the work of our meetings my group should:
(Groups, like individuals, pick up bad habits. If you were planning to run a training session for your group, what are the five lessons you would like to bring out?)

Obviously you can add other questions to this self-assessment and self-development exercise. For example, you may want to scrutinize your strengths and weaknesses as a committee member with a particular committee in mind. Surprise your colleagues by showing some enhanced skills at the next meeting. As always, build into your programme a self-review date. Never worry if your progress has not been as fast as you would like. Effort is always rewarded.

KEY POINTS: MANAGING MEETINGS

- Meetings are an inescapable part of corporate or social enterprise. Resolve to run them in a time-effective way. Begin by distinguishing between the five different kinds or purposes of meeting (see page 105).
- Becoming more cost-conscious about meetings will help you to be economical with time. Check if any given meeting is really necessary and ensure that people don't waste their time attending meetings if their presence is not required.
- Time spent on planning the meeting will repay itself tenfold. Work out the agenda carefully, allotting time for each item.
- As chairman you may be both referee and leader. Learn to distinguish between these two roles and blend them to perfection.
- Clear, concise and definite minutes are necessary. Although not always essential they should normally make reference to who is to do what by when and with a deadline time for reporting back.
- Only you can improve your skills as chairman or as an ordinary member of the group. Collect some feedback on your present performance, asking people to give some examples of your strengths and weaknesses to illustrate their general points. Then draw up an action plan to improve yourself over the next six months. Target some forthcoming meetings for practice purposes.

It is essential for the Cabinet to move on, leaving in its wake a trail of clear, crisp, uncompromising decisions. That is what government is about. And the challenge to democracy is to get it done quickly.

Clement Attlee, former UK prime minister

10

THE ART OF DELEGATION

Delegation has a strategic importance in the art of time management. Can you delegate effectively to others? Can you handle delegation when you are at the receiving end?

The importance of being able to delegate increases the higher up an organization you go. In a recent survey of 280 chief executives only thirty said that they could allocate time to correspond with the relative importance of the matters facing them. You can be sure that the other 250 were not good delegators.

What is delegation? It's vital to be clear about that. For many people still confuse delegation with abdication. To totally relinquish your power to someone else is not delegation. It is an evasion of responsibility.

True delegation is not like that. It means entrusting to another person a job together with the authority to do it. Thus the delegate now acts as your agent, like the emissary of a king. If you happen to be the delegate then a task or function is committed to you by someone in authority together with the necessary powers to carry it out.

DIFFICULTIES OF DELEGATION

Delegation as a necessary principle in organizations sounds simple, and so it is. What matters in organizations is doing such simple things well, but of course in organizations it is very difficult to do simple things well. Delegation is a prime example. Nothing in organizational life is more fraught with difficulties. It either doesn't happen enough or it doesn't happen well. Both sins of omission and commission consume rather than save time. That is regrettable. For good delegation yields a double crop to the acre: it allows you to conserve time for the key functions of your job and it also develops the abilities of your team members.

The trouble usually starts in the realm of attitudes and values, as the following comments made to me by managers at one international seminar on time management illustrate:

A senior executive in an engineering firm: 'Personally I believe that information is power. I prefer to keep the really important details secret from my staff. If I hand that over one of them might soon be able to displace me. When I was away sick for four weeks with my ulcers the whole place almost ground to a halt so you can see that I am indispensable to this firm now.'

Senior manager in a medium-sized company: 'I favour delegation in principle, but you should see the clowns that I have working for me. They are called managers but they are not up to handling novel situations that constant technological progress and rapid market changes are creating for us now. They aren't even properly trained. Most of them have psychologically retired even if they are not yet drawing their pensions. Now you know why I carry two bulging briefcases! I just don't know what to do about it. My boss – the managing director – keeps hinting that it's my fault, but I don't know what he expects me to do about it. He never tells me anyway what he expects of me.'

These are symptoms partly of genuine difficulties – those inherent in the process of delegation – and partly of lack of intelligence and skill in both delegator and delegate.

WHY IS IT DIFFICULT TO DELEGATE?

Research in five European countries has unearthed the seven top reasons why chief executive officers don't delegate. Can you add any other reasons (or excuses) to the list?

1. It's risky
2. We enjoy doing things ourselves
3. We daren't sit and think
4. It's a slow process
5. We like to be 'on top of everything'
6. Will our team members outstrip us?
7. 'Nobody can do it as well as I can'

WHAT CANNOT BE DELEGATED

A visitor to the Oval Office noticed a hand-lettered sign on US President Truman's desk:

THE BUCK STOPS HERE

Those four words summarize an essential truth. You can delegate authority to do a job and hold that person account-able to yourself for their performance. If you do it in the right spirit and in an intelligent way you will generate a sense of responsibility in the delegate. Responsibility can be shared. But you remain *ultimately accountable* for what happens – or does not happen – in your organization. If that burden is too heavy, remember President Truman's other saying: 'If you can't stand the heat, stay out of the kitchen.'

An important corollary of that principle is that at all times sufficient control of those under your management should be maintained in order to protect your ultimate accountability – this is a responsibility that cannot be delegated.

A manager is a leader in the business settings of industry and commerce. Leadership – the core of the manager's job – is the second responsibility that cannot be delegated. It involves becoming the kind of person and acquiring the necessary skills for achieving the common task, building a team, and developing individuals. These three areas obviously overlap: in most cases, for example, you will not achieve the task unless you build teamwork among your team members and colleagues.

The three areas of task, team and individual, together with the key leadership functions of defining the aims and objectives, planning, controlling, evaluating, team-building and developing individuals, are general in nature. They apply to *all* leaders in *all* walks of life. Of course leaders will have to share responsibility for their effective performance with others: there is too much required for any one person to do them all. But any leader worthy of the name will not delegate his or her key leadership responsibilities and functions to someone else. Otherwise he or she will be left with an empty title and a set of status symbols while the substance of the job has fled elsewhere.

EXERCISE 4: Chief executive

You are the chief executive of a large industrial organization in the electrical goods and electronics field, with a board of directors headed by a non-executive chairman over you. List the core responsibilities of your job: the ones that you feel that you must reserve for yourself although others can be called upon to help you to discharge them effectively.

Suggested answers – after you have completed your list – on page 172.

The essential responsibility of the chief executive – the main purpose of the role – is to provide leadership. Leaders should give a sense of direction: they must guide the organization in its way. It has to be the right way, otherwise they are misleaders rather than good leaders. Leaders should inspire, especially when difficulties and obstacles abound; they should energize and build enthusiasm into the organization.

Many parts of your job as a manager-leader can and should be delegated. But you cannot remove yourself from accountability and leadership. Lastly, you should never allow anyone else to take the decision on your behalf as to what you should delegate. That is your responsibility.

WHAT CAN BE DELEGATED

There is no set list of tasks that can be delegated. That depends upon several factors. What you can delegate in one case may not be possible to delegate in another.

It is a mistake to imagine that you either delegate or you do not. It is not as black and white as that. There is a continuum of delegation, depending upon the degree of control you wish to exercise. Some key points on it can be identified as follows:

DELEGATION CONTINUUM			
'Get on with the job; let me know what happened afterwards.'	'Get on with the job, but let me know if you need advice, help or support.'	'Get on with the job, but keep me closely informed of progress.'	'Don't take any action on this particular point until you have consulted me.'

In determining where to act on this continuum in any situation, you should take four factors into account. These can be seen as restraining factors, holding you back from delegating as fully as you would like. Therefore these factors need to be kept under constant review.

Factor 1: Confidence in team members

You are more likely to delegate if you feel that you can trust your team members. That involves a judgement on their professional competence and personal qualities. Able and well-motivated team members can obviously take the responsibility you give them; indeed, they will be frustrated if real responsibility and authority is not delegated to them.

The dangers to avoid are over-optimism and over-pessimism about any particular person. We all have our limitations. Some will do an adequate job, with little risk of anything contrary happening. Others need to work in harness with you. The best people are capable, sensible and well-informed, they fully understand the company's objectives and policies and appreciate the possible consequences of mistakes or errors.

For the chief executive or for a leader of equivalent level, delegation should be a way of life, not an optional extra. If he or she is to make it so, it follows that they must know key team members – and potential ones – exceptionally well. Therefore all systems of organization that divorce a leader from the people around and immediately below him or her must be counter-productive. How can you acquire and maintain that level of knowledge about people? For many good leaders it is a matter of intuition. But intuition can be a misleading guide. You need to spend time working with people, talking about them, observing them and reflecting on them until you form a sure judgement of how far you can delegate to them. And that degree may vary according to the particular decision, task or function that you wish to devolve.

Factor 2: Time available

As a general principle, the more you share decisions with others the more time it takes. The very time taken to explain and check understanding, providing sufficient information for the other person to act, may not be yours to give. Crises, where time is necessarily short – and where sometimes life-and-death issues are involved – do not favour the delegation of decisions, although paradoxically it is often then that having the capacity to delegate all but the most important activities can be most valuable.

Factor 3: Impact on the future

The increased demands on your time should compel you to set priorities and delegate 'whatever is time-consuming and not important', as one chief executive put it. The time–importance ratio is worth bearing in mind. You do not want to spend large chunks of time on the least important aspects of your job – and very little time on the big issues.

The natural candidates for delegation are therefore the more routine or administrative parts of your job. It is a mistake, however, to think that you can delegate *all* administration and concentrate solely on leadership. For organizing is one of the key functions of a leader. Routine may not be the most enjoyable part of your job, but in every vocation there is an element of toil. Accept the inevitable but essential attention to routine matters and their meticulous implementation.

At the higher levels of leadership, however, you must at all costs avoid getting over-involved in administration. The head of a large chemical company had the right idea when he explained: 'I delegate everything that can be defined. This leaves me to keep score on jobs that have been delegated and freedom to spend most time planning opportunities that lie ahead. As soon as jobs are defined, they will be delegated. My practice has been to select jobs I know best and could supervise most easily and delegate them first. Then as soon as the next job was defined and we could afford staff, it was delegated.'

In any position of responsibility it is vital to keep reviewing your present activities in order to see if any of them are ripe for delegation. 'I ask myself if anyone else can handle the problem,' a managing director told me. 'If so, it gets delegated. I am left with decisions no one else is in a position to make and follow up.'

Factor 4: Novelty of situation

Among wise senior managers there is wariness about delegating in areas where the company has insufficient experience to have formulated some guidelines for action. You should expect to hesitate longer before you delegate where the situation is so novel as to be uncharted. Negotiations regarding mergers and acquisitions could well fall into this category. It is the nature and delicacy of the assignment – not its complexity – that may make you feel that you must handle it yourself. Where there is a lack of definition, and much uncertainty, coupled with potential major consequences for good or ill on the profitability or development of the organization, do not delegate the matter to anyone else. Being free for such challenges or opportunities is an essential part of your job.

The primary purpose of delegation is to enable the organization to be effective, which it cannot be if it is a one-man band. The right approach is to assign tasks or functions to others though you remain immediately or ultimately accountable. The measure of authority necessary to perform has to be given too, subject to the degree of control – see the 'Delegation continuum' table on page 127 – that you agree with the team member. But delegation is also a powerful tool for developing the confidence and abilities of team members: it helps them to grow in stature. The art is to delegate just beyond the present capacity of a person, so that they are fully stretched. 'I use delegation as a powerful motivational weapon,' says one marketing director.

Obviously there is a balance to be struck between the needs of the company and the development needs of the individual. Many senior managers can identify with the chairman of an Australian mining company who wrote: 'I took over from two successful chairmen who had left too much to others – maybe because of outside interests. The process of curtailing powers and functions already engaged in has been difficult. My basis for delegation is to ensure that I am not landed with major unforeseen consequences.'

Many managers in industry and their equivalents in other organizations just cannot bring themselves to delegate more. They want to do everything themselves. If there is a problem to be solved, they must solve it. They do not delegate because they do not *want* to delegate. Often they are workaholics, who have risen by sheer hard work. Trouble starts when such people are promoted to the level of their incompetence. Large organizations soon lose momentum when there is a poor delegator at the helm and all large decisions – and even relatively minor ones – have to be taken by the head person alone.

The following case study illustrates these points. What are seen as strengths in any manager – the ability to work hard and the willingness to accept responsibility – can become failings unless balanced by other factors. The admiral who reverts to being a glorified gunnery lieutenant is a familiar type in all organizations. He works non-stop; details attract him like iron filings to a magnet. But people interpret his behaviour as lack of trust in them. Certainly such a person does not develop a management team or grow worthy successors.

Case study of a bad delegator at work

'Those dear devoted blockheads steamed steadfastly on through the night. They would have died for Jellicoe. But they would not send him a signal.' So wrote John Winton in *Jellicoe* (Michael Joseph, 1983), his biography of Admiral of the Fleet Earl Jellicoe, describing the Grand Fleet captains on that confused night off Jutland on 31 May 1916. They had just fought a bloody but inconclusive action against the German High Seas Fleet and looked forward to another – perhaps a glorious Trafalgar – the next day.

But it was not to be. Though the enemy had been sighted

many times in the night nobody told Jellicoe in time. At dawn, the North Sea was empty. It was Earl John Jellicoe who had to bear the brunt of the nation's disappointment.

Favoured by Admiral Lord Fisher, who had 'heavenly feelings' about his protégé as 'the future Nelson', Jellicoe had been appointed over the heads of twenty more senior admirals. In 1911 Admiral Sir Francis Bridgeman, whose promotion to First Sea Lord from Commander-in-Chief Home Fleet gave Jellicoe his chance, wrote to Admiral Lord Fisher: 'Directly I go, up he comes automatically to command of the 2nd Division [Second-in-Command of the Home Fleet] and a splendid opportunity for him! He has had no experience of fleet work on a big scale, and is so extremely anxious about the work on it, that he really does too much. He must learn to work his captains and his staff more, and himself less! At present he puts himself in the position of, say, a glorified gunnery lieutenant. This will not do when he gets with a big fleet. He must trust his staff and captains, and if they don't fit, he must kick them out! I am sure you will agree with me on this view, and I wish, if you get the opportunity, you would drop him a hint. He would take it from you, but perhaps not from me.'

This was a shrewd summary of Jellicoe's most serious fault: his unwillingness to delegate. Although Fisher must have had opportunities to help Jellicoe, he does not seem to have taken them. One of Jellicoe's great flaws remained his inability to delegate. Promoted to First Sea Lord in 1917, Jellicoe was a sad sight. This dedicated and gifted man gradually deteriorated under the strain of overwork, weariness, irritation with politicians and poor health. On Christmas Eve 1917 Jellicoe was summarily dismissed from his post.

DEVELOPING YOUR SKILLS AS A DELEGATOR

Delegation is an art in the sense that it requires considerable skill to do it well. Just as artistry transcends craftsmanship so true delegation rises above the communication skills needed to allocate tasks to others. Both parties feel by intuition that it is right; the creative dimension in some form or another is there. Start with the basic skills and after considerable experience delegation will become second nature to you. The following table should help:

SKILLS OF DELEGATION	
SKILL	**NOTES**
Selecting the right staff	'There are no bad soldiers – only bad officers.' It is no excuse to blame failure on the quality of your staff. You chose or accepted them. If they are too incompetent or unwilling to do the job, even with training, you should get rid of them. Selecting the right people is the foundation of delegation.
Training and developing the individual	However high the potential of your key staff – those to whom you wish to delegate – they will need training. Remember the training cycle: 1. Demonstrate job with delegate alongside 2. Get feedback and comment from him or her 3. Get delegate to do job and observe 4. Delegate does job on own – delegator available to answer questions 5. Delegate does job and reports back on completion. Start with small routine tasks and build up to challenging tasks as confidence on both sides grows.

SKILLS OF DELEGATION (cont.)	
SKILL	**NOTES**
Briefing and checking understanding	Both the training process and subsequent delegation require considerable two-way communication skills. What is being delegated must be clearly defined; the authority to do it must be spelt out. Others involved also need to be informed. Check understanding. Make sure the person knows the wider context: company aims and policies. Then he or she will know why it has to be done and how.
Standing back and supporting	Resist temptations to get involved. Do not rush in and countermand a team member's orders. If he or she comes to you, try not to provide the answers but help him or her to find them. For your aim is to develop the initiative of the team member and delegate. Then he or she can cope with problems, including those caused by his or her actions, as well as you have done in the past.
Controlling in a sensible and sensitive way	No one likes to feel that there is no rope connecting him or her to the anchor. Check progress at agreed points – see the 'Delegation continuum' table on page 127. Always remember that abdication is not the name of the game. Control is the essence of delegation.

If you are the delegator it is always helpful to put yourself mentally into the shoes of the delegate. Remember the words below, of a manager looking back on his early days in an insurance company:

At the end of a long day when I rose from my chair there were times when I used to kick the wastepaper basket under the desk just to relieve my frustration. As I went off home to an examination syllabus in which at least I was

master of my own fate I would mutter my prayer to the
departmental management:

> *Tell me what you want me to do and why*
> *Then let me get on with it*
> *If I make a mess of it kick me hard*
> *So I know where I went wrong*
> *BUT DON'T FUSS*

From the delegate's point of view a delegator who fusses
continually is a nightmare. Needless bustle or excitement,
a state of agitation especially over details and an undue
concern for niceties – the hallmark of a fussy nature – often
go hand in hand with the kind of person who tends to
be irritable and easily upset. Anthony Eden, Winston
Churchill's successor as UK prime minister, was a fussy man
in this sense. He found it difficult to delegate beyond the
ways the system required. If he did so he was on the
telephone to the unfortunate minister at all hours of the day
and night, restlessly busy over what appeared to any competent party member to be mere trifles. He certainly lacked an
even temper. No wonder that Churchill, on the eve of his
resignation, concluded that Eden was not up to the job of
being prime minister. But by then it was too late.

The crucial importance of creating and sustaining a climate of trust in modern organizations should now be clear.
Certainly delegation cannot work properly unless there is
mutual trust, founded on personal and professional integrity.
Trust is the oxygen of human relationships. Of course you
must earn trust by your abilities and contribution, your
reliability and trustworthiness. But trust has still to be given
to you as well, and not withheld for the wrong reasons.

'Confidence begets confidence,' says an old Roman proverb. Delegation as a gift of trust will generate an answering
trust. It will also generate self-confidence in the delegate.

Therefore it is an important leadership act towards creating a climate of trust in any organization. It is worth remembering that people are often better than they think they are and will always respond to a challenge – if it comes from the right source.

Once trust is tarnished it is hard to restore it to its original glow. Therefore do your best to keep it bright. The best way to do this is to stick always to the truth, for truth and trust are sisters. A senior colleague said of media tycoon Lord Thomson of Fleet: 'His most memorable quality was his instinctive habit of telling the truth. His strength, which was very great, particularly in dark moments, made him enjoy truth when another man would have found illusion more comfortable. He always faced reality and he always believed that he could do good business in terms of the reality that he faced.' Such integrity is the golden quality of leadership as illustrated in Lord Thomson's case study below.

A good delegator at work – Lord Thomson of Fleet

We had been given fair warning about the need for diversification and in Thomson Publications we did not appear to waste any time about it . . . we saw Gordon Brunton off to Australia to have a look at some trade and technical periodicals. I remember he came to see me before leaving.

'How do you want me to handle it?' He was still a new boy after all. 'Would you like a survey by telex or to wait till I get back and report to you?'

'You will find half a million available at the bank,' I said. 'If you see anything worth buying, buy it.'

This was the way I invariably trusted my executives. I believed they could do most things as well as I could, if not better, and I always avoided the mistake of kidding myself to the contrary . . . A man must not only know how to choose his executives, he must know how to delegate authority. Lack of this ability shows not only a lack of trust in the individuals themselves but a failure to trust and back one's own judgement. Many of the business failures I have known about throughout my life have come about through this. A man who cannot delegate to others finds himself without the time or energy to concentrate on essential problems. Nor will he be able to take the kind of decisions that are active, immediate and effective. I had also found that it paid to give an executive that confidence right at the start of his career with me.

Gordon was quickly successful in Australia and bought for us a group of the right kind of periodicals . . .

Lord Thomson of Fleet, *Long After I Was Sixty* (Hamilton, 1975)

Delegation, then, involves a calculated risk. Rational management practice quite properly tries to reduce the margin of risk in decision. There is nothing intrinsically meritorious in taking risks for their own sake. But reducing the margin of risk too slavishly may strengthen the centralizing forces upwards and further the bureaucratic tendencies in large organizations. The true delegator accepts the risk of delegation and its consequences because the alternative would, in the long run, be most costly and damaging.

You may wonder how Thomson would have reacted if Brunton had failed in Australia. Later in the book there is a story that suggests a possible answer. The editor of a leading British newspaper under Brunton was offered what appeared to be Benito Mussolini's diaries. After a six-figure payment had been made, some research established beyond doubt that the diaries were forgeries. Thomson recalled:

I was in Gordon's room, asking 'What is the news?' when he told me. It was a substantial sum that had flown with the confidence men. Gordon recalls that I then asked: 'How much would we have made if the diaries had turned out to be genuine?'

He told me – It would have been the publishing coup of the century.

'Well,' I said, 'It was worth taking the chance.'

I then asked him if he would have someone look into my driver being paid overtime for taking me home in the evening. Was that necessary and right?

It is interesting to speculate what Thomson would have said – had he still been alive and owned the *Sunday Times* – in 1983 when the company repeated the same mistake over the so-called 'Hitler Diaries' . . .

Unlike many heads of organizations, Thomson resisted the temptation to become a back-seat driver. Self-discipline was always at his command. Decisions, major as well as minor, were left to those he trusted. His chief executives, Gordon Brunton in London and others close to him, felt a sense of purpose in belonging to the Thomson Organization, though some of them could have moved to more financially rewarding posts; he was not a lavish employer. As we have seen, he stood by them even when, as sometimes happened, their decisions turned out to be wrong – provided they were wrong for the right reasons. Then no word of reproach came from him.

A true entrepreneurial leader will expect others to act like entrepreneurs and back them up if the risks do not come off. He spreads the belief that to a large extent you can make your own luck. 'My idea of luck,' said Lord Thomson, 'is that it is an opportunity seized.'

Because he delegated, Thomson could always find time, in the midst of heavy preoccupations and crises, to consider lesser topics, and to switch his mind to an altogether different perspective.

Lastly, through delegation Thomson grew managers of stature. Sir Gordon Brunton became chairman of the International Thomson Organization in his place, and in his turn proved to be an outstanding business leader.

KEY POINTS: THE ART OF DELEGATION

- Delegation begins with a deep sense of the value and limits of your own time. From that stems a strong desire to focus on priorities – the work that only you can do – and to delegate the rest. That will leave you free to think, plan and act effectively.
- Delegation is not abdication. Some degree of control needs to be maintained. The more trustworthy the team member, the less that will be.
- Managers often complain that they are running out of time when their team members are running out of work.
- Delegating the more routine or predictable parts of your job is only the first step. Giving people power to make decisions and to act in your place within a given sphere is the next one. That is not always easy. It requires courage, judgement and faith in others because you remain accountable for what they do.
- Exceptional tasks – those that are absolutely vital and that only you can be sure will be done in time and to the required standards – shouldn't be delegated. Nor should those where confidentiality or particular sensitivity is essential. The new, vague or ill-defined task may not be suitable for delegation either, for a delegate will waste too much time and effort trying to decide how to proceed.
- You should delegate some of your 'positional' authority to team members, matching the task you have given to them. But – like you – they will have to rely more on the

authority of knowledge and the authority of personality to get things done. Make sure you increase their knowledge and confidence.

• Delegation is a great motivator: it enriches jobs, improves performance and raises morale.

You will never have so much authority as when you begin to give it away.

11

MAKING USE OF COMMITTED TIME

Glass bottles and cardboard boxes can be recycled. Why not time? Of course time is not like these resources in most respects. But you can recover some committed time from the 'scrap heap' – the destination of those scraps and margins that are left over when a job doesn't quite fit the time available for it.

Committed time is time given over to specific purposes. Things we have to do and places we have to be: these take up much of our time. The aim of this chapter is to suggest some ideas about using off-cuts of time during these committed periods.

In many such situations there is some time when you are not actually doing what you have committed the time for: spare minutes or even hours when you're waiting or not fully occupied. For example, the person you are meeting may be late or the car isn't ready after a service at the garage and you have to sit in the reception office twiddling your thumbs. Or the dentist is running behind schedule, leaving you contemplating a pile of rather weary-looking magazines. If you are a master of the art of time management you can make some constructive use of these potentially wasted minutes.

For instance, this is an age of travel. You may be travelling constantly. Travel provides many opportunities for saving time. Waiting at airports or stations can be seen as a necessary evil. Or you can turn waiting to good ends and write a letter or read a book.

Redeeming committed time is a daily challenge. Look upon it as such. Imagine that the system will be playing against you; everything will conspire to make you waste time. See if you can cheat the system. Snatch some small victories today.

DAILY ROUTINES

Sometimes you can put time committed to routine daily essentials to a second use. Most actions repeated daily, such as walking, become habitual. Your unconscious mind, which is like a personal computer in this respect, takes over and runs the activity. Your mind is more-or-less free to attend to other things. Therefore time spent on daily routines can often be the first place to look.

Take getting dressed each day as an example. A pure efficiency expert might get out their stopwatch and ensure that you spend the minimum amount of time on this daily routine. But you may *like* dressing. Or you may want to do it in a relatively leisurely way so that you can think about other things. One friend of mine, working towards a business degree, records notes onto a tape recorder and plays them back while dressing each morning; you could do the same digitally or by using a dictaphone. Another friend's wife is using the same method to brush up on her Italian before going on holiday, with audio tapes and CDs now common tools in the home language-learning market. Shaving time can also be remarkably productive in ideas.

Daily exercise is another routine with time-use potential. One author of phenomenal bestsellers had a reading stand on his exercise bicycle. Other people watch TV or DVDs while running the treadmill – for many, this is a good time to catch up on the news, while getting fit at the same time.

If I can air a personal preference, breakfast ought to be eaten in complete silence. That happy rule certainly prevailed in the Scots Guards officers' mess in which I spent some of my national service days. Places were laid some distance apart in order to inhibit any attempt at conversation. On my first day I made the mistake of saying a cheery 'Good morning' to a senior major. 'Good morning, good morning, good morning,' he growled back, not glancing up from his copy of *The Times*, 'Now let that last you for the rest of the week.'

Meal times illustrate the theme of this chapter perfectly. The primary use of meal time is to eat and drink. Yet from time immemorial human beings have made meals social occasions, gathering with families and friends to converse together. It is perhaps the oldest and most familiar example of using committed time in a secondary way.

In monasteries and on religious retreats where meals are still eaten in silence, passages from edifying books are read aloud. If the extracts are well chosen this can be a valuable exercise in getting two benefits for the price of one. A home alternative, assuming the absence of chattering children, would be to have the occasional meal when books can be read in silence at the table. With this end in mind it is worth acquiring or making a reading stand. Don't make reading at the table habitual, however. Home meal times should also be about time to catch up with loved ones, family and friends – and of course, to eat.

After meals comes washing the dishes – a practical and mindless activity but one that somehow satisfies your conscience that you are *doing* something. If you don't have a dish-washer and are still washing the pots, use this time to let your mind take wing. British industrialist Sir Alastair Pilking-ton is said to have had the key idea that led to the invention of float glass while watching pots and soap in the kitchen sink. While the author Agatha Christie once declared: 'The best time for planning a book is when you're doing the dishes.'

Redeeming committed time

In one of his letters of advice to his son, dated 11 December 1747, Lord Chesterfield recalled: 'I knew a gentleman who was so good a manager of his time that he would not even lose that small portion of it which the calls of nature obliged him to pass in the necessary house, but gradually went through all the Latin poets in those moments. He bought, for example, a common edition of *Horace*, of which he tore off gradually a couple of pages, read them first, then sent them down a sacrifice to Cloacine; this was so much time fairly gained.'

Other physical activities, especially if they are more or less habitual, can also serve in the same way as washing the dishes. Bathing, walking, driving, riding a bicycle and gardening are all times when creative people report having ideas or making decisions. The poet Lord Alfred Tennyson had so many ideas while bathing that he had a special boiler installed in his house so that he could take hot baths at any time of the day. Find your own place to think in this way and you will find that your depth mind can help work out a problem, mysteriously relaying answers, solutions and choices to your consciousness like a computer.

Scores of people have experienced these creative breakthroughs or intuitions while engaged in daily routines or just relaxing. A British Nobel prize winner, Dr Godfrey Hounsfield, made the crucial breakthrough that led to the development of the body scanner while walking the Cumbrian fells. 'I'm very keen on rambling,' he said later. 'It's a time when things come to one, I find.'

WASTING TIME

Another type of committed time already mentioned is *waiting time*. For most people, waiting is simply a write-off. With a little planning and resolve, however, you can squeeze all sorts of activities into the minutes you spend waiting for the hairdresser or doctor or train. You can plan tomorrow's work, write a letter or pay a bill. You can even meditate or reflect, as recommended in the next chapter.

Waiting time, in an airport lounge for instance, gives you some bonus minutes of solitude if not silence. Be prepared for them by having the right frame of mind. As the dramatist and philosopher Goethe once said, 'Solitude is a wonderful thing when one is at peace with oneself and when there is a definite task to be accomplished.'

TRAVEL TIME

Travelling time has already been mentioned as a prime target – something you can make further use of. As a schoolboy I commuted to London every day for five years, a journey of an hour each morning and evening. I learned then the value of travelling time, for most of my required homework could be done on the train.

Arnold Bennett, author of *How To Live on Twenty-Four*

Hours A Day, writing in 1907, pictured the plight of the typical commuter: 'He walks to the station in a condition of mental coma. Arrived there, he usually has to wait for the train. In hundreds of suburban stations every morning you see men calmly strolling up and down platforms while railways companies unblushingly rob them of time, which is more than money. Hundreds of thousands of hours are thus lost every day simply because my typical man thinks so little of time that it has never occurred to him to take quite easy precautions against the risk of its loss.'

Reading newspapers on trains struck Bennett as a major time-waster. Although he read five English and two French dailies, he objected to reading newspapers on the morning train. 'Newspapers are produced with rapidity, to be read with rapidity. There is no place in my daily programme for newspapers. I read them as I may in odd moments. But I do read them. The idea of devoting to them thirty or forty minutes of wonderful solitude is to me repugnant. I cannot possibly allow you to scatter priceless pearls of time with such Oriental lavishness. You are not the Shah of time. No newspaper reading in trains!'

Anthony Trollope achieved his prodigious output as a novelist by writing his book on trains. As an employee of the General Post Office he was obliged to travel widely around the country over a period of years, and he put his time on trains to good use.

Long flights can provide similar opportunities. All air travel tends to be fragmented. Short-haul flights may save time in one way, but it is harder to get any work done on them. At airports, however, you will usually find some waiting time available after check-in.

Travelling man

Sir Terence Beckett, a leading British industrialist, believes in
the value of train travel:

'You have a table in front of you and you can spread your
papers out and really get on with the job in a much better way
than with your knees under your chin in a car or, worse still,
with your elbows clamped to your sides in an aircraft.

'I look forward to train journeys with real pleasure. By air,
your air travel time is only a small part of the total. It's getting
to the airport, hanging about and all the rest of it. With rail
you spend your time on the train, not constantly sprinting
from one place to another.'

Valuing his interludes of privacy, Sir Terence does not
approve of using telephones on trains. Nor does he ever take
a secretary along.

'To me, one of the great pleasures of going by train is that
they can't get you on the phone ... The chief advantage is to
get away from them all and to get on with it yourself. I don't
get enough time to do that.

'You can start thinking about things that in a busy life –
and that's what mine has been for all my career – you don't
get the chance to think about. You do get some very good
ideas as a result, especially on people and organization that
you've really meant to think about for quite some time. When
you come back you make decisions that perhaps you ought to
have made before. A train journey is almost structuring in, if
you like, a bit of time to think.'

TELEVISION

When Arnold Bennett's typical commuter arrived home he
had no radio or television to tempt him. An hour or so after

getting back he reported that 'you feel as if you could sit up and take a little nourishment. And you do. Then you smoke, seriously, you see friends; you potter; you play cards; you flirt with a book; you note that old age is creeping on; you take a stroll; you caress the piano . . . By Jove! A quarter past eleven. Time to think about going to bed!'

Radio, television, the telephone, computers and the Internet have revolutionized that Edwardian evening. Many people now look upon the evening as time committed to television. I am a keen watcher of television. I am obliged to mention this personal fact lest I should be accused of a prejudice against television when I say that committing the whole evening to it is a terrible waste of time.

If the television set is on for one reason or another, why not do something else at the same time, like reading a book or making a list of activities for the next day. Let your subconscious mind filter the television programme for you, so that you glance up or take notice when something interesting is going on. The invention of the remote control is an invaluable aid here: all the commercials, for example, can be shown without sound. Or you could invest in a digital TV service that allows you to schedule your own television shows – you decide what to watch and when, plus you can skip the adverts at the same time.

KEY POINTS: MAKING USE OF COMMITTED TIME

- You have to commit time, but not all committed time is used. Become aware of time as a piece of cloth that you are constantly cutting into shape. Pick up the off-cuts, the pieces of marginal time, and make use of them.
- Review your daily routines. Simply because they are rou-

tines – habitual and settled ways of proceeding – you may find that your mind could be active if stimulated by, for example, a recording of some notes you need to memorize.

- Waiting time, be it long or short, can be a positive opportunity rather than a negative time-drag. Become a wait-watcher!

- When choosing the most time-effective method of travel take into account the quality and quantity of the work you will be able to do on the journey.

- Review the amount of time you devote to watching television or surfing the Internet – if necessary cut down on quantity. Also, for most programmes, reduce the quality of your attention. You can do something else while half-watching, such as reading a book, drawing or writing a list of tomorrow's key tasks.

We all find time to do what we really want to do.

12

ON HEALTH AND HOLIDAYS

You may think it strange to find a chapter on health and holidays in a book on time management. What is the connection between the subjects? Why include it?

There is one obvious reason: if you are ill it is an interruption to what you are doing. Time may not be exactly wasted while you are recuperating, but it is certainly channelled into another use. A reasonable, positive and effective interest in your health is like taking out an insurance policy against illness that threatens to rob you of time that you would rather spend in some other way. Prevention is better than cure.

A deeper reason, however, concerns the *quality* of your time. Most books on time management concern themselves solely with the quantity of time you have available to you. They seek to persuade you to work longer hours by getting up earlier and by cutting out distractions or time-wasters. They frighten you with constant reminders of how little time is left. But they seldom address themselves to the fundamental issue: how can you increase the *quality* of your time? The aim of this chapter is to answer this question.

Imagine that work – your expenditure of energy and time in purposeful activity – is like a football match. What happens off the field, before the whistle blows, is vitally important to the outcome of the match. Are the players fit? Are they relaxed and confident? If their physical fitness and mental condition, especially their morale, is not good they are unlikely to produce high-quality football. So it is with you. However knowledgeable you are about the techniques of time management you will not gain the most from your time – the essence of the art – unless you are feeling physically and mentally fit. How can that be achieved?

YOUR ENERGY BALANCE

One of the major foundations of this book is the analogy of time to money. You could apply the same metaphor to energy. But there is an important difference. Nature is capricious. Everyone is born potentially with the same amount of time; energy comes in variable quantities. You have a quota of it. Wisely used, it can last you a lifetime.

In this respect energy does compare to a bank balance. Your money could be left to stagnate. Or you could add regular sums to it, building up your capital over the years. In many ways it's possible to be fitter in your fifties than at forty. You can be reasonably energetic well into your eighties, given some luck and if you have invested in your energy capital.

What is your energy? It is best defined as power expended or capable of being transformed into work. Work, of course, is not necessarily the same as paid employment. Energy shows itself in vigorous action, forceful utterance, strenuous exertion and vitality.

Tycoons – businessmen of exceptional wealth and power – like all others who have a passion for work, necessarily need an extraordinary amount of energy to fuel their furnaces. Many a talented young manager has failed to become a tycoon simply because he or she wasn't built to take the daily grind. 'It becomes clear pretty soon if you can't do the job,' said one entrepreneur to me. Another successful businessman made the same point: 'Thoroughbreds are bred to race. It's the same with people. It's something that's inborn.'

Thoroughbreds, like all other kinds of work horse, have to sleep, eat and exercise – and that applies to you too. The reservoir of your energy is fed directly from these three sources. Here is some commonsense advice under those three headings.

GET ENOUGH SLEEP

'Sleep that knits up the ravell'd sleeve of care,
The death of each day's life, sore labour's bath,
Balm of hurt minds, great nature's second course,
Chief nourisher in life's feast . . .'

Shakespeare's words in *Macbeth*, above, capture both the mystery and the properties of sleep. No one understands fully why we must sleep and what happens in sleep. But it is clear that sleep is essential for our physical and mental wellbeing. In other words, sleep conserves and restores our energy.

Individuals vary as to how much sleep they need. Some are 'Napoleons' who can manage on as little as three hours a night. This is very rare. Most people can *occasionally* manage on three hours' sleep a night. It is the average requirement that you should look at and that usually becomes less as we grow older.

It is important to discover roughly how much sleep you need each night and keep to it. For example, Archbishop William Temple, a man of wide-ranging interests and phenomenal accomplishment, was an exceptionally good manager of time. From his religious upbringing in childhood he had imbibed the idea that it was sinful to waste time. In between official functions and in various spare moments he composed books and wrote letters. At the height of the Second World War, when he was Archbishop of Canterbury, he ended one letter: 'I must stop now and get to bed, as I am writing out of my sleep.' Doing anything 'out of your sleep' is to be avoided if at all possible.

Former British prime minister Margaret Thatcher, who found that she could exist on very little sleep each night, still had to learn the same lesson. She decided in 1984 to burn less midnight oil and to restrict the amount of work she did in the small hours of the morning. Instead she maintained her workload by spending more time studying her papers before breakfast. The change stemmed in part from concern at the strain on her eyes from too much late-night reading. 'I now find it far better to apply a fresh mind in the morning rather than reading long hours into the night,' she said.

Some people are plagued with insomnia. The first remedy to this is to remember that we all sleep more than we think we do. So try not to worry about lack of sleep, unless insomnia really begins to affect the quality of your life and then it may be wise to consult your GP for advice; sometimes insomnia can be a symptom of another problem such as stress. Secondly, get up and do something. Or, if you wake early, you could lie in bed and apply your mind to a work problem. You will recall that this is the principle of moon-lighting, in the context of this book (see page 82).

If it suits you, take cat naps during the day – although this isn't advisable if you are not sleeping well at night. Edison and Einstein – two of our greatest inventors and scientists – both made a nap part of their daily routine. Churchill, Truman, Eisenhower and Kennedy are examples of political leaders who used naps as a means of maintaining their energy levels and coping with the pressures of high office. Check yourself against the following questions:

- Do you know how many hours' sleep you need on average each night?
- Have you suffered from insomnia at some time in the last six months? If so, what were the causes?
- Do you regularly go to bed too late at night, leaving yourself tired and irritable in the mornings?
- Have you tried taking cat naps during the day?
- Are you over-sleeping? Could you now manage with an hour's less sleep a night?

A BALANCED DIET

Today we are bombarded with advice from all sides on the subject of what to eat and drink, and our lifestyles. Many of these shots of advice fail to hit their target. For example, most people are now well aware that smoking can give you lung cancer, not to mention heart disease and a host of other illnesses. But despite public smoking bans and widespread anti-smoking campaigns in many countries such as the US and UK, the advice to quit smoking is still ignored by a significant part of their populations.

One difficulty in the diet field is that not only are there more experts, they tend to change their minds as new research becomes available. One minute we are told to avoid carbohydrates such as potatoes and bread; the next we are told that we need these fibrous foods to keep our diet balanced. Everyday it seems that we are presented with a new diet or nutritional plan to stay fit and healthy: 'only eat protein', 'cut out sugars', 'lose the fat', they say. Faced with these often discordant messages it may help to follow these three rules:

1. Resolve now whether you are the kind of person who lives to eat, or one who eats to live. If you are of the second kind, simply read on. If you live to eat – gourmet or glutton – then your values are different. Gourmets and gluttons need to set their food-loving values against their health and decide if their eating habits are having a negative impact. Too much rich food or alcohol could cause obesity or heart disease for example. Mould your values to your health: if you are passionate about eating out, why not try to adjust your restaurant and menu choices so that your diet is still balanced; if you love burgers, try making them yourself from fresh ingredients.

2. Take note of any consensus or general agreement among dieticians or nutritionists. For example, there is now a clear and accepted agreement in favour of a balanced diet. This cites that we should eat at least five portions of fruit and vegetables every day. Everyone – meat eaters, vegetarians and gourmets alike – can try to stick to this rule. Common sense, aided by a little instruction from the experts and a good dollop of self-knowledge – some people may not be able to eat certain foods for reasons of health or belief, for instance – is your best guide.

3. Remember the golden rule: *nothing in excess*. Cream, butter, sugar, alcohol and other suspect foods are usually fine if taken in moderation or occasionally. In some cases, research has shown that controversial items such as chocolate and red wine are actually good for us, in small doses and within a balanced diet. Conversely, consuming all the products of a health food shop immoderately and without the correct advice has the potential to harm your digestive system.

TAKE EXERCISE

Exercise is almost as contentious a field as diet. But the same basic principles apply. First, you must establish your priorities. Exercise is important for all of us, but some people *are* busier than others. *You* need to work out how much time you can spend on exercise and plan your time accordingly. Even if it's only thirty minutes three times a week you will have met recommended health targets. Look at your time log and see where you have been wasting time; you could use this time for exercise. Or refer to the previous chapter about using already committed time. You could work and exercise at the same time – just think of how many deals are struck on the golf course or what thoughts your depth mind could trigger while running at the gym. For exercise generates energy, despite consuming it in the short term. You shouldn't be living in order to exercise, like some fanatics, but taking exercise in order to live more fully.

The second rule of looking for the consensus points among the experts is easy to apply. All experts approve of exercises such as tennis, golf, walking, swimming or cycling, although they too need to be done with certain a level of care, instruction and personal limitation. These are activities that make you breathe deeply and increase your heart rate. The heart is a muscle that likes exercise. The respiratory and digestive systems are fellow beneficiaries when you walk briskly, swim or cycle. Therefore you would be wise to find some form of exercise that you enjoy and invest some time in doing it two or three times a week. It will both increase your efficiency and help you relax.

The third rule – nothing in excess – applies to the craze for jogging or excessively going to the gym. Jogging immoderately on hard surfaces can lead to damaged knees, ankles and backs; it can also – quite literally – be a way of running away from problems or other tasks in hand. Are you guilty of spending too much time at the gym? The sudden rush of endorphins released when exercising can give you a fantastic natural high, but too much exercise can paradoxically leave you with an equivalent low when you are not able to get your fix. Again, the words 'balance' and 'moderation' are key.

Warming up and, as research now shows, warming down – stretching after exercise – are also important. Plus try to avoid sudden bursts of vigorous exercise. Showing off on the squash court after months of inactivity, tackling a triathlon or marathon without training, or attending an advanced aerobics class, can all be potentially fatal for the unfit business executive.

Regularity is also important. Exercising three or four times a week gradually brings the heart rate up. Brisk walking is always good exercise; so is gardening or anything else that involves stretching the arms and legs. It is important to move the body and use the muscles in this way, for that keeps your body supple. Enjoy whatever form of exercise you choose – then you will keep on doing it.

'It is a fact,' said the writer Max Beerbohm, 'that not once in my life have I gone for a walk.' He could not have known what he was missing. Walking has much to commend it as a form of exercise. You can do it anywhere and you do not need any special clothes or equipment.

Apart from perhaps setting aside some time for walking in the countryside at weekends, you can also find opportunities for energetic walking each working day. It is the same principle as walking up or down the stairs rather than taking the lift – the value of the extra exercise is worth the expenditure of a little more time, for exercise is the vital principle of health and you ignore it at your peril.

'Yes, yes,' you may say, 'but I haven't got time to take

exercise in the regular way you are recommending. I am too busy tackling all those goals and objectives I have identified as a result of reading your book.'

If that is what you are feeling, it may be worth thinking about the answer Olympic gold medallist Sebastian Coe gave to suggestions that intense concentration on athletics may have narrowed his life.

The price of fitness

I hear a lot of talk about the great sacrifices involved in running, but personally I think it's a matter of organizing your time efficiently. I can run in the amount of time most people spend watching television. It's been worked out that the average person spends about three to four hours watching television every night. Well, in one and a half hours I can do a hell of a lot of good work. If that's missing out, it doesn't worry me. If running means not going to night clubs, not drinking excessively and not smoking, that's fine. I don't like that sort of life anyway.

Sebastian Coe, Olympic athlete

Sebastian Coe broke the 800-metre world record at the Oslo Olympics in 1979 with this kind of self-discipline. If he could run for ninety minutes a day, surely you and I can exercise a mere ninety minutes a week in order to be fit for daily living?

THE IMPORTANCE OF HOLIDAYS

Don't become a workaholic! Working hard is not the same as working long hours. If you do have to work long hours over a period of time, compensate by working less hard when you can. Friends, family and recreation are worth your time. Get your priorities right and maintain them. Symptoms of work addiction include refusal to take a holiday, inability to 'switch off' from thinking about work, and family members and loved ones who are practically strangers to you. If that is happening to you, you need a holiday.

What constitutes a good holiday is fortunately a personal matter. Ask yourself: 'What was the most memorable holiday I ever had?' Its ingredients – travel, friends, history, food, sun, beaches, mountains, sport or whatever – may be a relative guide when it comes to planning your next one, subject of course to the law that variety is the spice of life. With holidays, change for change's sake is sometimes a good thing.

If you are a time-conscious business executive or a professional person daily managing your time with care, reflect on the writer J.B. Priestley's definition of a holiday: 'A good holiday,' he said, 'is one spent among people whose notions of time are vaguer than yours.'

Holidays were originally holy days, extra days in addition to Sunday that were set aside so that people could remember the great events or saints of their religion. Holidays now are both secularized and largely commercialized. Perhaps we need to return to that fundamental idea that holidays are a time for mental and spiritual recreation, not merely for regimenting our bodies with a change of air and diet. For the quality of our time may depend as such on the state of our minds as upon the condition of our bodies.

Leisure hours in the evenings or at weekends are holidays in miniature. Many occupations provide plenty of mental exercise and stimulus. Should your job fall into that category, however, you may yet consider doing things in your leisure hours or during your holidays that will use other parts of your brain, such as learning a language. In my companion book *Effective Decision Making* I have given some guidelines for becoming and remaining mentally fit. This is as important as physical fitness, as health industry experts now agree.

PRACTICAL MEDITATION

The fruits of prayer and meditation were exemplified in Archbishop William Temple. Humility, he once said, is 'not thinking little of self but in not thinking of self at all'. Temple had the highest freedom available to a person, namely the ability to live each and every hour without fretfulness or anxiety. He once said, very characteristically, 'What wears one out is not what one does but what one doesn't do.'

In the Christian tradition prayer and meditation are linked. Prayer can be understood by analogy as a familiar conversation with God. The decline in religious belief in the West – along with a wider understanding and appreciation of the world and its customs through increased travel – has played its part in the popularity of meditation from countries such as India and China.

Yoga and other forms of Eastern exercise and meditation – aimed at the body and mind – are no longer unusual practices in Western countries such as the UK and US. Classes aimed specifically at busy executives are even commonplace today, often taking place one-on-one or on the office premises so that they are easier to attend. New forms of meditation are being invented all the time as practices and preferences are fused. While books on meditation and spiritual exercise are many, making it easy to find a style that suits you whether done at home or with others.

One of the first meditation programmes to achieve popularity in the West was Transcendental Meditation and some people still follow this method today. It involves sitting silently for twenty minutes twice a day, eyes closed, letting your mind wander where it will while silently repeating a *mantra* – a repeated phrase of Sanskrit origin. Practitioners say that TM makes you more alert and less tense. Some physical changes, such as altered brainwaves and slower, deeper breathing, are also said to occur. Research like this has brought TM many fans and paved the way for other forms of meditation. Our ability to 'switch off', especially in times of increased communication and long work hours, can no longer be taken for granted. Relaxing or even sitting quietly doesn't necessarily come naturally. Today, many people need help or guidance – in the form of meditation or similar – just to re-learn how to switch off.

The secret of Mahatma Gandhi

More than any other worker, the leader must lay up and safeguard reserves. Gandhi is a good illustration. He impresses one as being very frail physically. Yet where is there a leader subjected to greater strain? I think I found the secret of his wonderful endurance when I visited him at his Ashram near Ahmedabad. The only day on which I could arrange my crowded programme so as to step off to see him turned out, as I discovered on arrival, to be his day of silence. He graciously invited me in writing to sit with him during the period which terminated shortly after dusk. We then had a memorable conversation under the stars as he lay on his couch in front of his cottage. Among other things I asked him toward the close of our interview to tell what led him to observe a day of silence. He replied that he was so tired of talking and of hearing others talk. He found that in the tremendous pressure upon him he was not only breaking down physically but losing mental freshness and spiritual power, and was in danger of becoming formal, mechanical, and devitalized. He craved quiet for thought and prayer. And so he resolutely observes one day of complete silence each week. He told me that someone had asked him whether he would not break the silence in order to talk with the Viceroy, and he had replied that he would not do so for any person.

Sir Richard Livingstone, classical scholar

As the above passage makes clear, a key factor in all meditation is the need for silence. 'Turn aside and listen,' says the teacher. 'Sometimes you'll hear a quite different voice to those which assail you all day long. Let the babble of the human menagerie die down.' Quietness and contemplation go hand in hand. If you wish to meditate your first objective must be to create a time-bounded silence. It may be ten minutes early in the morning or late at night or an hour of walking by yourself or sitting on a river bank fishing. But the essential point is that you are alone and things are quiet. 'Silence is good medicine for the heart,' says one Chinese proverb.

Although you should not aim to bulldoze your thoughts in any one direction, meditation should be a purposeful activity. It is not the same as wasting time, still less killing it. You need to take a thought, an idea or a theme and gradually nibble away at it like a caterpillar on a cabbage leaf.

You could take the theme of this book – or some particular facet of it – as the subject of your meditations for a week. Take any three thoughts, words or phrases from this book. Write them down on plain postcards. Set aside ten or fifteen minutes before breakfast each day, beginning tomorrow.

Some people find it helpful to meditate with a pencil in hand, jotting down any thoughts that come to them. Think of the thought or phrase as a diamond that you are holding up to the light, looking into hidden flaws or fissures, turning to see each new facet. It is a journey of discovery, in which the ordinary discloses the extraordinary.

At the end of your three meditations, you may at least be more deeply aware of some aspect of time. You may be more conscious of it as a mystery or more grateful for it as an unexpected gift. Meditation is beginning to work for you. No effort; no reward.

So far I have been suggesting that you should meditate in a fairly structured way, selecting a subject and deliberately choosing or creating times when you can be alone and quiet. Meditation can be done in less structured ways.

Perhaps a better name for it would be reflection. Something said to you, some event, a thought-provoking sentence in a book, the changing seasons, the music of family life: any of these may start you thinking. We sometimes picture thinking as a kind of hard labour – mental work that produces a sweat on the brow. And so it can be. But in solitude, relaxing by the fire, glass in hand, thinking can also be a kind of play: an enjoyable exploration of some vein of meaning in your life. Such reflections may yield you moments of insight or deepen your values or warm your feelings, but even if they do not they are worth entertaining for their own sake. The fruit will come.

Reverie of this kind has been called 'the Sunday of thought'. It is a good idea to spend some time just meditating in this relaxed way about what you are doing in your work at present, even if it is only for a few minutes each day. The British businessman and journalist Walter Bagehot once said, 'No great work has ever been produced except after a long interval of still and musing meditation.'

Time to think

At some stage during the day, often during the evening, I make time for an hour's meditation. I sit in an armchair, perhaps with a glass of whisky, and consider what's going to happen tomorrow. I think of what the importance of it all is. I think of family things.

What it does is to put life into perspective. Something which at 10am seemed a terrible worry is no longer a worry when viewed in the context of what life is all about. I think that's why I'm a placid person. For some people a small event can become an obsession. Meditation stops one being constantly impetuous and in politics that's important. Leo Amery first advised me to meditate and now having done it for 16 or 17 years I couldn't do without it.

I never worry about what the future holds in politics. I take things as they come, otherwise there's too much to worry about. First you worry about becoming an MP; then you worry about becoming minister of state; then you worry about becoming secretary of state, chancellor, foreign secretary or prime minister. And when you reach any of those positions you worry about losing them. If you are crazy enough to do that you will not enjoy politics.

Peter Walker, former British politician

Practical meditation of this kind can change your life. Spiritually you need such times of silence and solitude. The French philosopher and mathematician Blaise Pascal wrote: 'All the troubles of life come upon us because we refuse to sit quietly for a while each day in our rooms.'

COPING WITH STRESS

John Smith is jolted awake by his shrill alarm clock. It took him a long time to get to sleep last night and he still hasn't shaken off his throbbing headache. He won't be going into work today and his absence, along with that of thousands of others, will have been caused by stress.

Stress was once defined by the *Oxford English Dictionary* as simply pressure or tension. It now includes a definition that alludes to 'a state of mental, emotional, or other strain', with the further inclusion of the word 'stressful' to indicate a cause of mental or emotional stress. Stress, it seems, is all around us.

Accepted research and studies on stress have now shown that it can cause a myriad of conditions from skin disorders, stomach ulcers, high blood pressure and headaches to nervous breakdowns and even heart attacks. Are you suffering from stress? The warning signs include:

- Disturbed sleep
- Constant tiredness
- Incessant worry
- Increased use of alcohol
- Excessive smoking
- Impotence or frigidity
- Over-eating
- Reliance on sleeping pills
- Drugs
- Irritability
- Lack of appetite
- Nausea
- Fainting spells
- Tendency to sweat for no obvious reason
- Insomnia
- Nail-biting
- Nervous 'tics'
- Frequent crying or desire to cry
- Headaches
- Backache
- Frequent indigestion

Many managers only recognize stress when they or an employee reach a crisis. This may be in the form of alcoholic dependence or a nervous breakdown.

Look at the situation in a positive light if you can. Stress symptoms can be 'friends' warning us to re-examine our life-style – the self-diagnosis can be: 'I need to take a searching look at myself and my career.' What concept do you have of yourself and of the time–change continuum – how much time do you have to change your ways? The need is to develop a philosophy of life that embraces body, mind, spirit, career and relationships.

There are times, however, when stress invades our lives like the sea surging over the natural barriers of sand dunes and man-made sea walls, as in the case study below.

When stress becomes a real pain in the neck

Sheila Henderson was looking forward to the New Year. Aged fifty, without children of her own, she had an interesting job working with a group of unemployed young people. Her husband Michael was a senior market-ing executive with a large pharmaceutical company. For eight months she had been nursing her mother at home, which she found exhausting. Suddenly, a week before Christmas, her mother suffered another stroke and died in the ambulance taking her to hospital; Sheila was hold-ing her hand. Two days later, her husband Michael received a curt note from his new chief executive saying that his services would no longer be required in the New Year. That same evening the police telephoned to say that three of Sheila's teenage trainees had been involved in a drugs party and had assaulted an elderly woman on a housing estate. The day after her mother's funeral was a Saturday, a day when Michael and Sheila usually played golf. 'You go ahead,' she said, 'and I'll join you later.' But in the kitchen, after Michael had left, she collapsed with an agonizing pain in her neck. She could hardly move. Doctors eventually diagnosed worn discs and advanced arthritis and told her that there was no cure. Two years later, however, when the causes of stress had eased, so did the pain in her neck.

The story of Sheila Henderson illustrates how stress is cumulative. It's not just one situation but continual stress that can lead to problems. A relatively minor event, when added to a large existing stress burden, can be the proverbial straw that breaks the camel's back. So if it's feasible, space out your changes as much as you can. Often, however, you won't have control over the kind of events that can head the list of stressors: the death of a husband or wife, the death of a parent or child or close friend, a marital separation or parting from someone you love, illness or injury, major changes at work or the loss of your job. So your objective then is to adapt your response to them.

The onset of serious stress symptoms may not be so sudden and dramatic in your life as in the above case, but the physical signs of pressure, anxiety and depression can be equally worrying. If this is the case, the obvious first step is to consult your doctor to ensure that there is nothing fundamentally wrong. Then you need to follow the 'Seven Steps to Counter Stress' on page 168 to cope with this unwelcome visitor; this seven-point plan covers both external and internal factors.

Sensible time management tackles the twelve most common roots of management stress. Research on 1,000 managers in ten countries – reported in *International Management*, May 1984 and still relevant today – identified these as follows:

1. Time pressures and deadlines
2. Work overload
3. Inadequately trained team members
4. Long working hours
5. Attending meetings
6. Demands of work on private and social life
7. Keeping up with new technology
8. Holding beliefs conflicting with those of the organization
9. Taking work home
10. Lack of power and influence
11. The amount of travel required by work
12. Doing a job below one's level of competence

For one or more of the reasons given above, stress can break through your sea defences. What can you do to manage or control it? If you are already experiencing some symptoms of stress here's what to do about it:

SEVEN STEPS TO COUNTER STRESS	
1. TAKE ACTION	Regard the symptoms in a positive light, as early warnings. Identify the underlying stress factors and do something about them. For example, if you are unhappy at work take stock and look at other options open to you, such as retraining or applying for a move. Any action is better than brooding. Go for a walk or take some other exercise. Smile and respond cheerfully, despite your feelings.
2. EXPRESS YOUR FEELINGS	Avoid isolation. Try to communicate with others. Don't bottle up your feelings. Find a way of expressing your anger and hostility, if that's what you feel. Talking to a friend or spouse might be the answer. Or you may have to seek professional help from a doctor, pastor or counsellor.

3. REVIEW PRIORITIES	Stand back and take a look at your values and priorities. You may be suffering from self-inflicted wounds. A fresh vision of your priorities in life can clear your mind of confusion and stress. Balance work with recreation. Abandon the all-work, no-play ethic.
4. ACCEPT WHAT CANNOT BE CHANGED	Seek the courage to change the things that can be changed and the serenity to accept the things that cannot be changed – and the wisdom to know the difference.
5. PUT YOUR EXPERIENCE TO GOOD USE	Put the negative experience to work in some way or other. Thus you redeem it. That means turning a minus into a plus. For example, use your own suffering to become more sympathetic to others who are going through the mill.
6. CHECK YOUR TIME MANAGEMENT SKILLS	Don't accept or set yourself unrealistic deadlines. Remember that too tight a programme for the time available is the major cause of management stress. Review all your time management skills where you suspect that you are weak, such as delegation. Allocate more time to your important tasks. Work and act methodically, doing one job at a time.
7. COUNT YOUR BLESSINGS NOT YOUR AFFLICTIONS	Concentrate on the present. Avoid dwelling on past events or future uncertainties. Gratitude is your greatest ally. Make a list now of five things for which you can be truly thankful. In your meditation this week, see if you can add five more blessings to your list.

Worry is always a potential enemy, especially when you are feeling tired. When it assails you remember the writer Mark Twain's words: 'I have known a great many troubles, but most of them never happened.'

KEY POINTS: ON HEALTH AND HOLIDAYS

- Conserve your energy and build your health by following sensible guidelines over sleep, diet, exercise and holidays. Remember that the golden rule is *moderation*.

- Practical meditation requires the simple ingredients of silence and solitude. Take some time each day to reflect upon things. You may wish to meditate in the classical sense of feeding upon some truth or value. Or you may like to reflect upon the deeper agenda of the day. Are your priorities right? Are you missing some blessings in disguise?

- Learn to recognize the symptoms of stress and to diagnose the underlying factors. Apply a seven-step strategy for coping with stress if it invades your life: take action; express your feelings; review priorities; accept what cannot be changed; put your experience to good use; check your time management skills; and count your blessings, not your afflictions.

- If you are worried, focus the object of your worry as definitely as possible in the camera of your mind. Ask yourself: 'What's the *worst* that could come of this? Can I cope with *that*?' If you can answer those questions, the nagging worry will usually vanish.

- Live one day at a time. You can't change what occurred yesterday. You can make tomorrow better by living well today.

> *Lord, there's never enough time for everything*
> *Help me to do a little less a little better.*

SUMMARY: TEN STEPS TOWARDS BETTER TIME MANAGEMENT

1 Develop a personal sense of time
2 Identify long-term goals
3 Make middle-term plans
4 Plan the day
5 Make best use of your best time
6 Organize office work
7 Manage meetings
8 Delegate effectively
9 Make use of committed time
10 Manage your health

ANSWERS

EXERCISE 4: CHIEF EXECUTIVE (page 126)

Suggested answers:

1. Ensuring that the organization has a sense of direction, expressed in clear aims and objectives. (Does the board of directors and senior managers know where the organization is now in relation to its competitors and markets and where it wants to be in three years' time? Does it have vision?)

2. Establishing a corporate plan, flexible in nature that will lead to the attainment of those aims and objectives.

3. Deciding on priorities – the allocation of money and resources in accordance with aims/objectives and plans.

4. Determining major policies, the ones that will guide the decisions of managers further down the line. Major policies are those that establish or develop the value system to which the company will adhere.

5. Organizing, in the sense of determining the basic organizational structure, and selecting/developing the key executives.

6. Developing four or five potential successors in the context of developing a management team.

7. Building relationships with the chairman and board of directors.

8. Forging key external relationships within the industry, with major customers, with the community and with government.

9. Controlling, including the establishment of standards and the monitoring of performance, in order that the organization achieves its aims and objectives.

INDEX